W9-ALV-884

FRANZ KAFKA
MAN OUT OF STEP

Kafka photographed toward the beginning of his university years.

FRANZ KAFKA

MAN OUT OF STEP

by Deborah Crawford

WITHDRAWN
TPHS-IMC

CROWN PUBLISHERS, INC., NEW YORK

TINLEY PARK HIGH SCHOOL
TINLEY PARK, ILLINOIS
LIBRARY DISTRICT 228

921
ΚΑ
cl

ACKNOWLEDGMENTS

I am grateful for the assistance I received in gathering
material for this book from Mrs. Marianne Steiner, niece
of Franz Kafka, from Mrs. Dora Ziegellaub and Helmut
Galliner of the Leo Baeck Institute in New York, from
Mrs. Johannes Urzidil, and from Professor Fritz Bamberger of the Hebrew Union College–Jewish Institute of
Religion in New York.

The author gratefully acknowledges the Akademie der
Künste, Berlin, for the photographs reproduced in this book.

Text copyright © 1973 by Deborah Crawford

All rights reserved. No part of this publication may be repro-
duced, stored in a retrieval system, or transmitted, in any form
or by any means, electronic, mechanical, photocopying, record-
ing, or otherwise, without the prior written permission of the
publisher. Inquiries should be addressed to Crown Publishers,
Inc., 419 Park Avenue South, New York, N.Y. 10016.
Printed in the United States of America
Library of Congress Catalog Card Number: 72–79793
ISBN: 0–517–50075–2
Published simultaneously in Canada by
General Publishing Company Limited
First Edition

The text of this book is set in 11 point Times Roman.
The illustrations are black and white halftones.

For Dr. Egon Wissing, a book-loving radiologist who has been collecting the works of Kafka long before he was universally known, and who still keeps an eye out for signs of Kafka's continuing influence

Introduction

A FEW YEARS AGO a motion picture was made called *The Trial*. It was directed by Orson Welles and starred the actor Anthony Perkins. In it, a young man, while waiting for his breakfast to be brought in by his landlady, is visited by two police officers and told politely but firmly that he is under arrest. They can't tell him what his alleged crime is, but, in the interest of conforming with authority, he goes with them to headquarters. Threats of a pending trial and a prison sentence arouse in the young man a progressively more fearful sense of guilt—he must have done *something* to deserve this treatment. He seeks relief from his anxieties in the company of a woman who, while not objecting to his advances, is unable to help him understand his situation.

The trial never takes place, the prison sentence is never handed down; but finally, still not knowing what, if anything, he is guilty of, he is accosted by two other officials of the law who, just as calmly and dispassionately as the first two, proceed to murder him, as if he had actually been tried and found guilty of some terrible crime.

The movie was taken from a book also named *The Trial*, by Franz Kafka; and the main character, called simply "Joseph K.," was Kafka himself, for this was the way he saw his own life. The life was a continuing "trial" fraught with a deep and unnameable sense of guilt. It was a short life but an intense one, in which this man sought, desperately and in vain, for happiness and, perhaps more than that, for peace of mind. Yet in his futile searching he discovered something else—a vision of life that was strange and often terrible but always fascinating, and he began to write about people and happenings in a way that no one else had quite managed to do before.

He saw deeply into the hypocrisies and dangers of his social system in its relentless attempts to force every individual into conventional roles. Yet he was not what one would call a dropout; in fact, he tried to conform to society's rigid demands, with tragic results. He feared and despised bureaucracy—the established order—with its power structure, deaf to the needs of human beings, especially the poorer class. Still he did not join those who advocated the violent overthrow of the government. Instead, he wrote about these things. He wrote his protests, silent and nonviolent, against everything in life that was false or evil. And not as a journalist, crusading for better conditions, but simply as a man—a man of dazzling imagination and insight—setting down his troubled thoughts and dreams in order to at least free himself.

He did not write much—three short books, about eighty stories, some of them no longer than a paragraph, a diary, a notebook, and a long, impassioned letter to his father, which his father was not given to read. Only a part of one of the books and a handful of the stories were published in his lifetime. Yet the world now acknowledges Franz Kafka as one of the greatest writers of the twentieth century. His name has become a part of the language—a "Kafkaesque," or Kafka-like situation being one of a strange or nightmarish quality—his works are now studied in university courses, and the list of books and articles written about him numbers in the thousands. As a critic wrote recently, there were few writers of any time or place who exerted such fascination for the modern reader, or such compelling influence over his imagination, as "a neurotic, tubercular Czech Jew" who lived in Prague around the turn of the century, and who died there in 1924, age not quite forty-one.

Yet for all the unique fascination the stories exert, the real life of their author is every bit as strange and dramatic. This book is an introduction to that life.

One

> "Strip his clothes off!
> Then he'll heal us.
> If he doesn't, kill him dead.
> He's only a doctor, a doctor!"

THE BOYS OF PRAGUE chanted this ditty, running to and from the grammar school across the Old Town Square, and at least one of their number, Franz Kafka, didn't mind the fierce sentiments expressed, because that meant that at the moment his classmates were not interested in turning upon him.

> "Oh, be cheerful, all you patients,
> The doctor's laid in bed.
> In the bed, in the grave,
> Right in there beside you!"

The children had made up this song after hearing the remarks of their fathers, whose feelings about doctors were that if they couldn't save a man's life they should climb into the grave along with him.

They were a mixed group, the children of Prague, in the 1880's. There were the Czechs, mostly sons of farmers, who even at age six or seven were tough and strong; and the German boys whose fathers were shopkeepers or in the civil service and who were usually of a less sturdy build which didn't keep them from fighting with the Czechs on the slightest pretext. Franz Kafka was wary of both groups because he knew that he belonged to a third —a handful of boys who were considered to be neither Czechs nor Germans, but Jews. And much as the first two factions picked fights with each other, they were both of the Christian faith and would close ranks in an instant against a Jew. Just recently Franz had heard that some other boys had ganged up on a Jewish child. They had hit him across the forehead with a pencil box, so hard that now the boy was blind.

At age six, the boy whom the Czech children called "Frantisek" and the Germans, "Franz," was a very thin youngster, whose large gray eyes under a shock of black hair looked, in photographs taken at the time, usually a bit alarmed, as if to say, *What next?*

He had been born on July 3, 1883, in an apartment of a fine old house in Prague which was called *Zum Turm* —"By the Tower," because it was next door to a church. This house was just off the beautiful, historic Old Town Square, among whose ancient stone buildings and statues could be read a great deal of Prague's thousand-year-old

The house Zum Turm *where Kafka was born.*

history. The Kafka family soon moved to another apartment building nearby, which also stood next to a church. The Kafkas were unable to ignore the prevailing Christian atmosphere of Prague, since on Sundays, holy days, and during the May devotions to the Virgin Mary, the sound of great pipe organs and Gregorian chants reverberated throughout their rooms.

Franz was the first child of Herrmann and Julie (nee Löwy) Kafka. Two other sons, Heinrich and Georg, were born in the following two years but both died in infancy. From the beginning, Franz's nature showed a mixture of

Franz Kafka between five and seven years of age.

character traits from both the Kafka and Löwy families, and as he grew older it was apparent that he was being constantly pulled between them. Julie Löwy was a quiet, placid woman; her father had been a pious patriarch who loved most of all to sit around the house discussing fine points of Hebraic thought. Julie's mother, Esther, had died very young of typhoid fever; Esther's own mother, overwhelmed with grief, had gone out, ostensibly for a short walk, soon after the funeral, and drowned herself in the Moldau River. The Kafka side was very different. Franz's paternal grandfather, for whom he had been named, was a butcher who liked to demonstrate to the child his ability to lift a fifty-pound sack of flour off the ground with his teeth, and boasted at being called in by innkeepers to help them throw out gypsies, the boisterous, drunken Czechs who roved in packs.

Herrmann, Franz's father, was a big, barrel-chested man with a booming voice who was totally dedicated to his role as a proper citizen in the middle-class world of business in Prague. As a child, Franz was inspired by his father's towering presence and wished desperately to win his approval, but every effort led to the opposite, to ridicule and rejection. Franz was to write later that it seemed there must have been something missing in himself, some terrible lack that made it impossible for his father to love him.

Actually, Herrmann Kafka was a discontented man who could find little good in anybody. A Czech Jew from a dirt-poor farm family, he had grown up hard, with barely enough education to learn how to write his name. At age seven he had been sent to the next town to work in a store, where from sunup to sundown he pushed a wheelbarrow of vegetables from village to village. His legs were runny with open sores because his stockings were always wet from splashing in the muddy dirt roads. His family all slept in the same crowded room, and they were grateful if they could get enough potatoes to fill their stomachs. At age eleven Herrmann Kafka ran away from home. He made his way to Prague, determined to earn a decent living; but there, after several years of struggling, the young man who had always regarded himself as a Czech, realized he could not get anywhere in starting a business unless he learned a considerable amount of German. He had to be able to deal with, and "toady" to, the Germans, who controlled most of the city's interests. And so Herrmann Kafka toadied, and finally owned a drygoods warehouse where men's clothing was packed and shipped. But his boyhood in the country and his humiliations in Prague had left their mark. The father of Franz Kafka was, despite his material success, an embittered man.

His influence on his only son was to be great. And so was the influence of the city in which Franz Kafka lived for most of his forty-one years. Prague, with its ancient somber history, its dark, almost mystical fascination, shaped in some way its every citizen; and none more lastingly than the man whose writings were to mirror its cobbled streets, its gargoyled buildings, proud statues, bridges, and storied river.

Today Prague is the capital of Czechoslovakia, but in 1883 when Franz was born there was no such place on the map, and Franz Kafka—along with his fellow Czechs —was truly a man without a country. Prague was the capital of Bohemia, a vast, rich land which was part of the monarchy that Austria and Hungary had formed in 1867. It was not until the end of the first World War in 1918 that the monarchy was dissolved and Czechoslovakia came into being.

Founded in about 1232 around the great ninth-century Prague Castle, and spreading out from the hilly banks of the Moldau River, Prague in the 1890's was one of the most splendid and cultured cities in Europe. It also was unique in that culture, chiefly because of the nature of its population. The Czechs numbered about 375,000; the Germans, 28,000; yet the German-speaking element, thanks to the policies of Austria-Hungary's government, had a disproportionate allocation of the economic, political, and cultural positions. Czechs labored as farmers and manual workers; Germans were businessmen, civil servants, or students at the German University, where, because of their better education, they graduated into the professions. The Czechs, resenting the Germans on Bohemian soil, dreamed of a day of independence from Austria; the Germans, on the defensive themselves in this "land of gypsies," looked upon their neighbors as unlettered peasants.

But both Czechs and Germans—united in their Catholic religion—looked down on the Jews of Prague. Though born in the city, the child Franz Kafka was regarded by the Czechs as a German; and although he spoke and was taught German history and literature in grade school, the Germans regarded him merely as a Jew.

Why this prejudice against Jews? The answer is complex, but perhaps a part of it was their refusal to become integrated, to enter into the daily lives of other cultures in which they chose to dwell.

The oldest Czech chroniclers passed down legends dating back to pre-Christian, pagan times, when several gods were worshipped. A little band of Jews had been driven out of Russia and for ten years wandered as exiles until they reached Bohemia. There, years before, a princess had had a vision on her deathbed that such a group of wanderers, worshipping a single god, would seek protection in Bohemia and would bring their blessing to the land. And so they were welcomed and given shelter. The Jews multiplied and prospered but they kept to themselves and built a wall around their houses, their shops, and temple to shut out the corrupting influence of alien customs. Only when obliged to did they mingle with the community, but they kept to their own ways of worship, their own holy days, special mode of dress, education of their children, and their language, a corruption of ancient High German which was called Yiddish (Jewish). The walled place became known as the *ghetto* (derived from an Italian word related to "cannon factory," as it was on such a site that Venetian Jews had built the first such place). Compulsory ghettos, built by Gentiles for Jews, were not to come into existence until the fourteenth century.

As the Middle Ages unfolded the region of Bohemia gradually became Christianized. The Jews resisted Christianity as strongly as they had resisted the pagan beliefs; but the Catholic Church was a more powerful adversary. Now the Jews were forced to live only behind the ghetto walls they had erected, even though the houses and streets had degenerated into filthy, stifling slums. Next they were penalized by a "Jews tax," and made to wear yellow stars on their coats to distinguish them on sight; they could not send their sons to grammar school or the university, and only the eldest son in a family was permitted to marry, to hold down their population, and this only after the father's death. This repressive existence went on for centuries; and it was not until 1860, around the time that Franz Kafka's father Herrmann was running away from home, that the gates of the ghettos were finally opened and all prohibitions were lifted—for economic reasons. Jewish muscle and Jewish money were needed in the towns and cities that were burgeoning in the light of the new mechanized age of the Industrial Revolution.

But although Jews had been given freedom of movement, they were made to see, in every way, that they were still regarded as second-class citizens. When Herrmann Kafka was striving to establish his own business, he was aware that even his name had a humiliating association. For centuries Jews and Christians alike had never had "last names" but had called themselves by such titles as "Abraham Ben [son of] Isaac," or "John the son of the tailor." But by the year 1782 the population had swelled to such an extent that there were likely to be several sons of tailors named John in the same community; and the Bohemian government decreed that everybody should take a last name. The Jews refused, so after several years of hauling them into court the judges began assigning them names arbitrarily; and by the time the judges had argued with the most stubborn holdouts they began to assign the most insulting names they could think of, such as "Cellar-stairs," "Stinkweed," "Gallowsbird"—and "Kafka," which meant a jackdaw, a smaller version of a crow. A jackdaw is not a particularly attractive bird, but when Herrmann Kafka went into his drygoods business he had, somewhat defiantly, a handsome, glossy version of the bird drawn up and printed on his official stationery.

From as far back as Franz could remember, his father had told him about his troubles as a starving youth in the farm regions and his battles for financial success in the city. But the boy did not come to any grown-up, mature realization that his father's experiences had made him permanently bitter, suspicious, and disapproving. Young Franz felt that his father was disapproving of him alone.

In 1884 a writer named Olive Schreiner wrote: "The barb in the arrow of childhood suffering is this: its intense loneliness, its intense ignorance." Such was the childhood of Franz Kafka. One of his earliest memories was, as a very young child, lying in his bedroom, hearing the companionable voices of his parents in the outer room, and calling to them for a glass of water. As he wrote later with his painful sense of honesty, it wasn't so much that he'd been thirsty as that he wanted attention. His father had yelled for him to be quiet and stop pestering them. Franz persisted, and his father threatened to give him a thrashing. Still with a sort of despairing stubbornness, Franz kept calling for water. Finally his father stormed into the room, snatched the boy from his bed, carried him out to the apartment-house balcony and slammed the door behind him, leaving him there in the dark. Years later Franz still could not forget the sense of terror and desertion that this experience had given him. It seemed to prove that he was a mere nothing, and might be picked up and tossed out of the house at any time, for no reason at all.

Even after he began school at age five, events continued to convince the child that he was next to worthless. Every morning he was taken across the busy square by the cook. This cook, a hard-worked, homely little woman, perhaps annoyed by this extra duty, would threaten Franz that she was going to tell his teacher how bad and sulky he had been at home. Franz, whose strict upbringing had already made him painfully aware of the need to be "good" in his every action, would defend himself by saying that he hadn't been bad, only "sad," and not sulky but "not talkative"; but the cook still threatened to tell; and so they would cross the square, Franz holding back and near tears, the cook pulling him along. As he recalled, she never told on him, but every day she threatened to.

After school it was the Kafka family's maid who waited for Franz at the school door. Some days, to the boy's relief, she was late, and then he would run off in the opposite direction from the one she was likely to take, and join a group of slightly older boys. Franz had been jeered at by the boys in his own class because of being taken to and from school, and he was afraid they thought of him as a little Jewish weakling. He thought if he could be seen in the company of older boys, especially in the thick of one of their fights, his classmates would change their minds about him. And so Franz would clench his fists and strike out in the group's frequent street fights, but this usually ended in his being beaten up and coming home in tears, with a torn and dirty suit. The maid and the cook would then try to clean him up before his parents got

The house in which the Kafkas lived during Franz Kafka's schooldays at the Gymnasium.

home. At one point the cook called him "a little Rava-chol." This was a Czech version of the name of a French revolutionary figure. Franz asked his parents, playing cards in the evening, what the word Ravachol meant. His father said it had come to stand for a criminal, a mur-derer. The boy, in spite of his getting into fights, had a horror of violence, and he demanded an explanation from the cook, who said in surprise that she hadn't meant that young Master Franz was going to turn into a murderer! But after that, Franz gave up trying to join the bigger boys.

By the time he was six he was convinced that he *was* a weakling; his own father's attitude did this. Herrmann Kafka would brag of his own physical strength and robust health to the aunts and uncles who came to visit, and then would say something scornful about his son being a poor eater, that's why he was so thin, and got colds so easily, and ending with the barked command to "At least stand up straight!" Around that time Franz's father decided that it might help develop his body if he were taught how to swim. Franz was a bit afraid of the deep end of the "baths," the city's large swimming pool, but he went along with his father gladly, as up to then father and son had hardly ever done anything together. But Franz soon came to dread these outings, which were to go on all that sum-mer and for several years to come. At the baths it was the custom to change into one's bathing suit inside a small hut. Herrmann Kafka insisted on Franz's sharing his hut, and the sight of his father's naked body seemed to the boy nothing short of magnificent. Compared to it he felt his own small frame was a skeleton—a skeleton that would never grow and flesh out and become heavily muscled, like his father's. They would emerge from the hut, Herrmann Kafka holding his son's hand, and make their way past other bathers, Franz feeling that everyone must be wondering if this frail, bony child could possibly be the son of this powerful man—and yet despite his sense of shame and inadequacy, Franz, as he was later to record, was proud of his father's physique. Worse was to come as he was pulled into the water over his head, floundering and spluttering, trying to move arms and legs in obedience to his father's shouted commands. After half an hour Herrmann Kafka would burst out in irritation at the boy's stupidity, they would go back to the hut and dress, not speaking, and thence homeward, Franz in his familiar state of disgrace. Later, in his early manhood, Franz Kafka taught himself to swim and learned to enjoy the water.

One cannot help but speculate that a man such as Herrmann Kafka—materialistic, "physical," and self-made, would have set great store not only on his success in business and as a family man but also as a producer of sons, sons in whom he could see his own image. He had fathered three male children, but two had died in infancy, and the only one left was a thin, shy, introverted boy who had little interest in physical activities such as sports, and from the time, around age five, that he'd learned to read, was usually to be found in a corner of the house hunched over a book.

Three other children were born to Herrmann and Julie, the first when Franz was six. All three were girls.

The burden of being his father's only son remained on Franz's frail shoulders.

He was probably right in feeling that in his father's eyes he was an unacceptable son.

Two

By the time Franz was ten, the apartment in which the Kafkas lived was crowded with his sisters—Gabriele, Valerie, and Ottile—nicknamed Elli, Valli, and Ottla. Neither the cook nor the maid had time to pay Franz more than token attention, which suited him fine, as it meant that there was less criticism of him in the house.

His mother Julie was, for the most part, absent from Franz's earliest memories because, in the daytime, she worked as her husband's secretary in his warehouse office; but now that she had three young daughters to care for she was obliged to stay home. This didn't mean, however, that she was much more of a mother to Franz. One day, as the boy remembered, she gave him a *sechserl* (a coin

Franz Kafka, aged ten, with two of his sisters, Elli (center) and Valli.

worth about a dime), probably to get him out from under foot. Franz was excited; he'd never before had more than a couple of pennies at one time, and a *sechserl* seemed an enormous sum to him. He ran to the Old Town Square with visions of all the things he might buy with the money—penny candy, a whistle, a small paperback book—and then he halted at the sight of an old beggar woman. She was in rags and she looked hungry, and Franz was seized with an overwhelming desire to give her the coin. But then he hesitated, standing before her and shifting from foot to foot. It seemed that a whole *sechserl* was a sum that nobody perhaps had ever given to a beggar, so he was embarrassed to do something unheard of; yet give it to her he must! So he ran over to where a man was selling flowers, and got the coin changed into a handful of copper *kreutzers;* then he ran back and gave one of these to the woman. She thanked him and mumbled a blessing. Franz then started to run around the whole wide square, so as to arrive from the opposite direction as if he were a new benefactor—and gave the woman a second *kreutzer*. Again he started off on a run and came back to her and repeated his performance. He kept on running and reappearing with another coin, and still another, until he was dizzy and out of breath in his determination to give her all of the little coins—but somewhere between his seventh offering and his eighth the beggar woman, seeing the boy advancing upon her again, shuffled hurriedly away. As Franz was later to write, she had probably lost patience with him. He ran home then, exhausted, and blurted out to his mother how he had spent his money. Julie Kafka thought that was very generous of her son, and gave him another *sechserl*. A fresh problem for Franz?

When not in school, Franz spent a lot of his time in the old square, watching the comings and goings of the people of Prague: German students in high spirits staging mock battles on their way to the university; German officials striding by, pompous in their stiff black suits or gold-braided uniforms; Czech shopkeepers scurrying about on local errands, white aprons flapping in the breeze; Czech peasants jogging along with wagons piled with vegetables or squealing pigs or crates of fowl. At the stroke of the hour, the boy would lift his gaze to the bell tower, the world-famous *Orloj;* as the great bell rang out, he liked to watch the iron figures of the Twelve Apostles of Jesus, St. Peter, St. John, and the rest, marching with solemn slowness around the face of the clock.

Also he admired the lightning rod stuck to the top of a nearby tower. That, he knew, was the marvelous invention of the American, Mr. Benjamin Franklin. Already Franz was aware of America; his teacher, a very strict and demanding German, was making sure that young Franz and his fellow pupils learned at least a few phrases of English and some facts about that great and far-off country. Franz's teacher was more admiring of Mr. Franklin than he was of his language. "English is the language of commerce, so you who expect to make your living in business had better learn some of it," was his comment.

Franz had picked up some English phrases without any special trouble, and he liked to murmur them to himself as he stood around in the square, because words were beginning to interest him more and more, and these words sounded so interestingly strange.

But aside from the English phrases, Franz was finding his studies a matter of constant alarm. Arithmetic was the worst; he just couldn't make any sense of something called fractions; in fact, his teacher had held him up as the stupidest pupil in arithmetic, and called him a crocodile. Franz felt that if he could just go more slowly, and have some help from his teacher, suddenly the mysteries of arithmetic would become clear to him; but he did not have the courage to ask for help. In literature he was doing much better, and was often impatient at the slowness of others in the class; and even at the age of eleven or twelve Franz could see that the aim of his teachers was to erase any trace of individuality in a child.

To his own surprise, somehow he passed every year into the next grade, despite his teachers' railing at him for stupidity, and more frequently, inattention and daydreaming. Franz knew they were right about one thing, that he wasn't really interested in the ten hours a week of Latin and Greek required of every high-school boy, or in the history of wars and conquests leading to the formation of the Austro-Hungarian empire. All he wanted, he was beginning to realize, was to scribble down his daydreams. He felt guilty about this, as about practically everything else, but he continued to do it, for it was only when he was making up a story that he was happy.

The only bearable aspect of school was the hour a day devoted to singing—choruses and anthems, mostly, from the music of Bach and Beethoven. Franz responded to the splendor of these stirring melodies, and wrote later that

Herrmann Kafka's business in the Kinský-Palace (ground floor, right). *Kafka's Gymnasium was on the first floor.*

he felt as if he were beneath water, and the music was pulling him along like a fishhook.

And after school what beckoned? Why, the fact that the school which Franz now attended was a big old building called the Kinský Palace, a building that also housed his father's office. The elder Kafka had been complaining that he missed his wife's help in the office, since she now had the little girls to take care of at home—and also that Herrmann's three brothers—Franz's uncles, were always too busy, or thought themselves too fine, to help out. So

Franz, still trying to make friends, would stop in at the warehouse after school. But, all he would get for struggling to lift heavy cartons at his father's side was: "Nobody to help but a weak kid. Give that here, you'll drop it and break something."

In spite of this thankless reception, Franz kept going to the warehouse to do paper work or anything else his father cared to give him. But soon Franz began to dread these afterschool hours, because of the way "Herr Kafka" treated his employees. He shouted, cursed, and raged at them for being lazy, unpunctual, careless, and stupid. He was especially wrathful about one clerk who was frequently absent from work, and who had said he had tuberculosis and had begged not to be let go as he had a family to support. Herrmann Kafka kept the man on, but whenever he was absent he would rant about the fellow being a mangy dog, and the sooner he died, the better!

Franz couldn't help seeing how his father's tyrannical manner had made his employees fear and hate him, and this was hard to face, since the young man was still trying to see Herrmann Kafka as a figure of benevolence, wisdom, and justice—everything that a father should be. And so he tried to rationalize that it was only at work that he behaved in such a way, because of the strain and responsibility of running his own business. At home he was often jovial, tender to his wife, and generous with gifts to Franz and his three little sisters. Of course, that was only when everything was just the way Herrmann Kafka wanted it. . . .

That was the trouble, as Franz had to admit to himself;

it took only the slightest action or word on anybody else's part to send his father into a frightening rage. The battleground was often around the dining room table, and Franz the most frequent casualty. According to his father, every scrap of meat on the plate must be eaten! To Herrmann Kafka, food was not only precious but a symbol of his ability to feed his family. But his son did not share his gargantuan appetite. Still, night after night, Franz was supposed to eat the large chunk of meat, the whole potato, the dumpling, and the thick gravy ladled over it all; and, moreover, at a rapid rate to keep up with his father, who did not approve of conversation while eating, but liked to lean back in his chair afterward and, if in a good mood, regale his family with an anecdote or a joke.

Adding to the lack of appetite in this growing boy was his father's rage at the way the food had been prepared, calling it swill fit for pigs—the cook was a beast who had ruined it. He forbade anybody cracking soupbones with the teeth to get at the marrow, or sipping wine noisily, or cutting bread with a knife dripping with gravy, or letting scraps of food fall to the floor; and yet, Franz noticed, it was Herrmann Kafka himself who committed these lapses, as well as sharpening pencils and cleaning his fingernails with his pocketknife, digging at his ears with a toothpick, and cursing and swearing in front of Franz's mother and sisters. Franz felt that he was a slave, living under a master's laws that applied only to slaves.

And, like the lowliest of slaves to his master, Franz, by the time he was twelve and had formed some opinions of his own, realized that in the face of his father's opinions, any contradictions were strictly *verboten*. Herrmann Kafka's face would redden with anger and he would start fumbling at his suspenders with the intention of taking them off to whip his upstart of a son. He would, he shouted, tear him apart like a fish! From the doorway the maid and the cook looked on in fascinated horror at the behavior of their "fine gentleman employer"; and then it was the role of Franz's mother, the gentle Julie, to preserve order by promising her husband that if he let Franz off "just this one time," he would not venture to contradict his father again.

Thus Franz was saved a beating, but he did not appreciate his mother's intervention, since, besides emphasizing his own weakness before his father—a beating might have been better—she was tacitly assuming that he was in the wrong in whatever opinions he had. Around that time in his life he began to stammer and stutter whenever he considered saying anything at all to his father, and after that, he stopped trying to communicate with him altogether, because it had become impossible even to think in his presence.

His mother saw this and tried to draw closer to Franz herself; but Herrmann Kafka got in the way of any good relationship that mother and son might have established. When older, Franz understood that his father had been jealous of Julie's attention and affection toward anyone else, even—perhaps especially—toward her son. In the evenings after dinner, if Julie Kafka showed any indication of going off with Franz to talk or help him with his homework, her husband would quickly draw her into a game of cards, which would last at least until it was time for him to go to bed.

Franz Kafka's mother, Julie Kafka, nee Löwy.

Bedtime often meant another unpleasant scene. Franz was turning more and more to reading, perhaps in an attempt to escape from his own world into another, freer one. But neither Herrmann nor Julie Kafka were readers, and they had not the faintest idea of how important reading was for the boy; they saw him simply as a child who should be sent off to bed at a certain hour. Perhaps they were even slightly piqued at this precocious offspring who preferred above all other activities to bury his nose in a book. And so Franz would be told that it was too late for him to be up, still reading, that he was damaging his eyesight, he would be too sleepy to get up in the morning, and the trashy story, whatever it was, wasn't worth it. After Franz had protested they would turn off the gaslight and leave him in the dark, restless to know how the thrilling story ended.

However, there was one element in the Kafka household which was beginning to bring a ray of light into Franz's life—his three little sisters. Up to that year they had formed a noisy clan against their big brother, a situation which Franz noted later with a touch of wry humor. On the infrequent occasions when Herrmann Kafka had taken the family out for a Sunday stroll by the river, the girls would try to throw him into the water, while their father would look on with an indulgent smile and their mother would pretend that nothing was going on. Franz thought their attempts to push him into the Moldau were an indication that they considered him, as a male, "unnecessary." But their behavior might also have been prompted by their father's attitude. For, like Franz, from their earliest childhood Elli, Valli, and Ottla were forced to vie for attention and approval from the elder Kafka, and it may have seemed to these girls, who were growing up timid, malicious, and bad-tempered, that one less member of the family would work to their advantage. But by the time that Elli, the oldest, was six, they were all coming to Franz for advice on "what to do about father."

Up to then Franz had made some attempts to be friends by writing little plays for the children to act out. He was already keenly interested in all types of performing—the circus, traveling actors, early silent "flickers." The girls had taken to this idea with enthusiasm and would give "command performances" before their parents, with Franz content to play stage manager. But this small effort had promptly fallen through. Franz could see that something about it disturbed their father; he scowled, became restless, looked at his wife, and finally, waving at the small actors to go on without their audience, he would scrape back his chair and demand that his wife keep him company at cards. It was apparent to Franz and the girls that their father did not really want contentment at home, that he thrived on keeping them at odds with one another. Having agreed on what was wrong, they then tried to figure out the right way to inform their father of this fault, hoping he would "see" what he was doing and improve his behavior.

And so brother and sisters would seek out a quiet corner of their apartment after dinner and put their heads together. Tonight Herrmann had done it again, had come out with dirty expressions that had obviously embarrassed their mother. And how angry their father had been with Ottla for being chummy with the maid, and at Elli who was becoming vulgarly fat. As Franz remembered later, the four of them had huddled together not in order to plot against their father but, in a mixture of fondness, defiance, revulsion, and guilt—with an occasional hysterical burst of laughter—to try to figure out in their young, inexperienced way, how to come to grips with their father.

But one night while they were still floundering about with battle plans, Herrmann Kafka suddenly put his head in at the door and, sneering loudly, called them all conspirators against him. They were, Franz and Valli, Elli and Ottla, appalled. Conspirators against their own father! After that, they began to meet less and less, until the whole determination to confront their father dwindled to nothing.

Franz still sought out, from time to time, the companionship of his mother. Once in a while she would encourage him about his lagging schoolwork, or give him a little pocket money so that he could indulge in a new interest, horseback riding. At those times she would call him by his Yiddish name, Amschel, the same as her own father's. She told Franz what the name meant: "blessed, fortunate, or happy."

So far, Franz did not feel he was any of these.

Three

PUT A BOY OF TWELVE on a spirited horse, and send him down the country roads that abound outside the city, and no matter how badly things are going at home or at school he cannot be all unhappy. Add to the horseback riding an increasing skill at rowing a boat on the river, and swimming at the public baths, plus the writing of short stories, and the picture brightens by the moment. Franz Kafka was developing some hidden resources to help him surmount his general discontent, his essential loneliness.

Striking out with vigor in the big city pool, or floating lazily on his back he would spin stories in his head; they made fine company. In one early tale he saw himself as a hero having come back to his hometown from the Olympics where he had set a world's record for swimming. Everybody was at the railroad station to welcome him; a girl stepped up and put a sash over his shoulders that proclaimed his victory. The crowd called for a speech, and the so-called victor gave them one, extremely short, in which he confessed that frankly he could not even swim!

That small early story was an example of what was to come—Franz Kafka casting Franz Kafka in the role of principal player, but hardly as a hero. Another early attempt was an exception to that pattern. Here he imagined himself driving into the old Jewish ghetto as a rich man in a splendid carriage driven by four spanking horses, and with only a curt command, rescuing a beautiful young lady who was being beaten—unjustly, he added—and carrying her away with him.

At thirteen Franz made his Bar Mitzvah. During the service he was obliged to say, like every other young man in this ceremony, "Today I am a man." Later he had to recite a speech, memorized with difficulty, for the benefit of his family, relatives, and neighbors. His father berated him for making a poor showing.

At that time Herrmann Kafka represented himself to Franz as being an example of wisdom and piety in the Hebrew faith, although Franz could see that his father never read from the Talmud at home and only went to the synagogue three or four times a year, on the High Holy Days, and then spent most of his time discussing business with other men. But Franz was not a son to sit in judgment on his father—only on himself. He did not believe for a moment in the words he had been obliged to say, "Today I am a man." He did not think he would ever become a man in the sense that his father was. Perhaps, he mused, he would go from being a child to a very old, weak man, of whom nothing would be expected.

His own body had become a hostile stranger. It had shot up to a lanky height and now he hardly knew how to make it behave. His mother kept after him about slumping, and all Franz could manage in self-defense was that he didn't see how round shoulders could make much difference in his future. To correct his posture Julie Kafka decided that he should take dancing lessons. The prospect of presenting himself to strange girls as a dancing partner was well-nigh unthinkable. Adding to Franz's alarm was his father's decree that he should have a black formal suit to go dancing in. Franz protested that only funeral directors wore black. Then, said his father, it must be a dinner jacket. Franz said he wouldn't wear a dinner jacket and look like a "fop." His mother started to plead and his father to raise his voice, so Franz agreed to have a tailor come in and measure him. The tailor said the jacket would have to be low-cut which meant Franz would have to wear a stiff shirt. He didn't want that either, so he said he would agree to a jacket if it were buttoned high. The tailor said he'd never heard of such a jacket. Franz said he had seen one like it in a shopwindow. They all went across the square to the shop but the jacket had been taken out of the window, and Franz didn't have the nerve to go into the shop and ask about it. So the little party went back in a state of indecision, Franz enduring his mother's reproaches, his father's scornful remarks, and the silent contempt of the tailor. And it seemed to Franz that he had cut himself off forever from

Kafka at the age of fourteen or fifteen.

many experiences he would really have liked, given half a chance—from making an elegant appearance, and going to dances, and talking easily to girls.

Some of the boys in his class had already taunted him for his obvious lack of experience with girls. Mortified by this judgment of his peers, Franz laid the blame upon his parents, more particularly his father. They should, he felt, have instructed him in at least the rudiments of sex! One evening when Herrmann Kafka took Julie out for a walk, Franz asked himself along. Father, mother, and son strolled over one of the ancient bridges in the light of the setting sun, looking for all the world to see, the picture of a calm, contented family group. Franz, however, wished to air his grievance. Stammering as usual when faced with his father he brought up the subject of sex in a casual manner, as if it were only an incidental subject of conversation and of hardly any interest to himself. He ended his little speech with a light reproach at his having had to learn the facts of life from outside his family, and added that because of his ignorance he had been very close to dangerous consequences; but now, as a result of his friends setting him straight, he knew everything there was to know, and no longer was in need, thank you, of parental advice!

After having got this out of his system Franz felt relieved, and with an attitude of having forgiven his parents for their oversight, he declared that the subject could now be considered closed. But Franz's father paid no attention to his airy attempts to control the conversation. Herrmann Kafka proceeded to supply Franz with what he had said he had wanted—the facts of life. These facts were presented in the crudest manner and were followed with practical advice; for instance, where to go to procure any number of young women to relieve his sexual urges, and what to do to protect himself against the dangers of disease—disease that should under no circumstances be brought into the Kafka household. On and on went the brassy voice, pointing out the difference between "loose" and "virtuous" women; and Franz, who up to that moment had regarded women as individuals—appealing or not appealing, just as men were—was shocked at his father's brutally casual advice, not only because it dragged down his ideals, or that such excruciating details had to be mentioned in the presence of his mother (who walked at that point a little bit ahead of her husband and son) but because here again his father had no understanding of Franz's real need, his simple purpose of a light reproach which was to be acknowledged, man to man; and then the two, father and son, as Franz had hoped, would have been drawn closer by the son's own evidence of growing up.

What really bothered Franz in that experience with his father was the injustice of his behavior. By then he had formed a belief that the world consisted of ultimate truths, and it was a constant source of protest in him that everyone (himself the first and worst offender) continually fell short of those truths, or perfections. A father should act in such-and-such a way; a son also. Truth was also the preservation of life, in which Franz believed passionately. And justice; every man should be treated fairly by his fellowmen. Then there was beauty: Franz's whole being responded always and in any form to beauty, especially that which he found in nature.

He also had deeply felt beliefs about religion; he could not bring himself to believe in a personal God, although he wished he could; but he intended to study the Bible and the Talmud more, and learn Hebrew, and perhaps later he would change his mind. As for politics, being a Jew he could not make himself feel involved with the city's elections of mayors, invariably Christian; there was no country he belonged to; and he couldn't feel much sympathy with the Austro-Hungarian empire's wrangling with other countries; but he did feel stirrings of interest with the growing unrest of the Czechs, who wanted their independence, their own beloved country. Then there was science: Franz felt an instinctive disinclination toward most scientific facts. He had recently begun a notebook in which he put down his thoughts, more as company for himself than as future story material. In this notebook he "talked" with himself about science. It seemed to Franz that one could discover more about life's realities by observing people's behavior than by looking at specimens in the slides under a microscope. Yet for the rest of his life he was to be torn between his suspicion of science and his respect for it, as for example in his later admiration for the inventions of the American, Thomas Alva Edison.

And then, because even the writings in his notebook were not enough to satisfy his longing to communicate his feelings, Franz Kafka began, in those years before he went off to the university, to fill the pages of his writings with drawings.

They were small, simple pen-and-ink sketches of what today would be called stick figures. These figures, faceless, bloodless, were usually depicted in a situation of closed or cramped quarters, in which their limbs were constricted. And their attitudes were those of men of whom the American writer Henry David Thoreau had said, "lead lives of quiet desperation."

Hardly a more fitting example can be imagined to illustrate Thoreau's phrase, or those terse stick figures, than the life of their artist, Franz Kafka.

Four

In 1901 when Franz was eighteen he was enrolled at the University of Prague, founded in 1348 and one of the finest seats of learning in Europe. Overnight, his rather oppressive home atmosphere was, at least for the better part of the day, replaced by one that was almost exhilarating. He found many other young men who were interested in discussing new ideas, such as Sigmund Freud's theory of dreams, and Charles Darwin's scientific evidence that Man was probably descended from a close relative of an ape. Franz Kafka was about to come out of his shell.

Several of his classmates had moved out of their parents' homes and into rooms of their own; one or two wondered whether Franz would consider sharing such quarters. But Franz wasn't ready to shake off his family's yoke. Night after night he continued to go home to his father's noisy arguing at the dinner table, his mother's flustered attempts to keep the peace, his three sisters' squirming discomfort. Afterward he would take refuge in his room to do his homework, and try to write in his notebook or work on a story.

One wonders why he continued to stay on with the parents who seemed so "wrong" for him, when many other young men, younger than he and coming from less unhappy family situations, had elected to leave and set up places of their own. Part of the answer must have lain in Franz's stubborn hope that he could, even after all these years, still win his father's loving approval. And while he remained under Herrmann Kafka's roof he could be considered by society to be a son, and not wholly a man, ready to take on a man's responsibilities of husband, provider, and parent.

Soon his father was demanding to know just what Franz intended to do with his expensive university education. Franz, as usual, couldn't think of an acceptable answer. He mentioned his growing involvement with his writing; and got what he had anticipated—scorn. A Jew, he was told, should go into a profession, to earn the respect of all. Franz finally mentioned the word "lawyer," and felt the warmth, the never-before-known warmth, of his father's approval. He, Franz, would never lack for clients in Prague with the Germans who had the best positions and most of the money, and the Czechs who were always in need of a lawyer to sue their neighbors.

Franz fought against this a little; he was appalled at the

thought of having to get up in a courtroom and make impassioned speeches. He took a course in chemistry, thinking to go into a laboratory, then one in German literature; perhaps he could become a teacher. And then he gave in. He reasoned that since he couldn't spend most of his life doing what he wanted to do most, writing, he might as well go into the study of law.

Already Franz had developed a strong sense of justice, of right and wrong in human endeavors, and it seemed to him that at least he would find the satisfaction of seeing justice in action in a court of law. So he set himself to the task of studying lawbooks with all the diligence he could summon up. But it soon became evident, as he digested hundreds of pages of dry and torturous paragraphs dealing with matters of plaintiffs and defendants, torts and penalties, and writs of habeas corpus, that he was chewing on mouthfuls of sawdust that had already been thoroughly chewed by many, many others. He was being stuffed with this sawdust, and when the process was completed he would be firmly packed with the lifeless chaff, and then he would be a lawyer.

He found himself unable to sleep, but lay in bed for hours, watching the moon slowly move in and out of the clouds and feeling that his life had become unreal. Franz Kafka, Attorney-at-Law. What a joke! Sometimes he would laugh aloud in the darkness. It was better to laugh than to weep.

He continued his law studies in his second year at the university—what else was there to do? But at that time a new element was added to Franz's life that had been totally lacking before. He had not known how much he needed to fill the empty space caused by this missing element, until it was filled. The element was one which most people possess and take for granted; but with his lonely childhood and growing up, Franz had had to wait until the age of nineteen to find it. It was, simply and most importantly, a friend.

"Reading and Lecture Hall for German Students," read the sign over the door. Franz had entered the place, a clubhouse, rather hesitantly the first time, as membership was not open to "professed" Jews, that is, members of the recently formed Zionist organization, who considered themselves Zionists before Germans or Czechs. Franz wondered if he would have to prove he was not a Zionist, when actually he did not even feel much like a Jew. Nobody challenged him in the clubhouse, however, and he was easily admitted into the company of the other young men. It was Franz's first conscious attempt to make friends, although one would hardly have guessed this by observing his behavior. He would sit for hours at a crowded table, fastening his intense gray-eyed gaze upon anyone who happened to be speaking, and giving that man's words close attention. Perhaps once during the entire meeting he would venture a remark, in a quiet, rather apologetic tone, pointing out some other aspect of the subject in question, or making an observation in the form of a mild but fitting joke. Within a few weeks he began to realize that the others were listening to what he said; not only that, but if there was other conversation going, those speaking would suddenly stop so that they might hear what *he* had to say! This response was astonishing to Franz, after his years of being told in effect by his family, "Your opinions are worthless and not to be tolerated." One day at the club he heard an especially gratifying remark: "That Herr Kafka, he's hit the nail on the head again."

It may have been uttered by another law student by the name of Max Brod. Young Brod had been growing more and more interested in the observations of this fellow member who never opened his mouth unless he had something to say, something that had obviously been thought out carefully and over a period of time. This, Brod knew, was the rarest kind of person, a true thinker, a man any man would be fortunate to have as a friend.

Max Brod began falling in step with Franz as they left the club in the late afternoons. To his surprise and further appreciation, Brod found his quiet new acquaintance to be anything but taciturn, at least when in the company of just one other man.

Franz Kafka had found someone to talk to, and all his pent-up thoughts came rushing out, like the steam from a pot whose tight lid had suddenly been released. After a torrent of words Franz would stop on the street and face Max Brod with a stammering apology, whereupon Brod would burst into laughter. At Brod's side Franz strode briskly along, scarcely able to contain his joy; he had made someone else laugh, someone who enjoyed his company; this, then, was what it was like to have a friend!

They spent many afternoons of their summer vacation at the public baths. Stretched out on the sun-heated boards under the trees, they talked about everything: their mutual lack of enthusiasm for their law studies, their families, first meetings with girls. Gradually Franz let out his more private, deeper feelings that up to then he had confided only to his notebooks. He felt, for example, such respect and concern for language that he was fiercely indignant about using it carelessly, especially by swearing, which he regarded as a form of murder. Franz carried his passion for the use of language into discussions of literature, and there found a fervent disciple in Max Brod. They exchanged opinions and shared each other's literary discoveries. *This* recently published book by a famous author was trash despite all the critics' high praise; *that* article by an unknown writer was brilliant and daring.

But there was one subject that Franz never brought up —his own attempts at writing. His respect and admiration for good literature were so great that it didn't even occur to him to say, "I myself am writing stories," or, "I should like to become a writer more than anything else in the world."

During that same year Franz met, through Max, another man who was to become a good friend. He was Oskar Baum, of whom Franz had heard when he was a child—the boy who, at age ten, had been blinded by a blow on the forehead in a street fight. Oskar Baum had never regained his sight but he had grown into a resourceful young man, and while his friends were attending the university he had studied music at home and was now earning a living as a piano teacher. When Franz and Max got to the Baum house that day, Max introduced Franz Kafka; and as was the custom, Oskar Baum bowed formally in the direction of Franz's voice.

At the same instant, Franz also bowed. It may have seemed pointless to bow to a blind man who could not appreciate the gesture. But Franz Kafka never thought to make any exception in his courteous treatment of all men. As it so happened, Oskar Baum realized that Franz had bowed, because in the gesture the two men's heads had very slightly grazed. The knowledge that he had been bowed to made a profound impression on the blind Baum. As he told Max Brod later, Kafka had been almost the only person in all his years of blindness who had treated him as a normal human being, and showed him that his "deficiency" was something that concerned nobody but himself.

Franz's consideration of others was shown to his friend Max in another incident a few days later. He had dropped in to visit Max, and as he strode into the living room, Max's father, who was taking a nap on the sofa, half-awoke at the sound of his steps. Instead of apologizing or explaining his presence, Franz simply held up a calming hand, and walking on tiptoe past the reclining man, said in a low, gentle voice,

"Just think of me as part of your dream."

Such gestures as soothing a sleeper or bowing to a blind man were admittedly slight, yet their long-term influence was not overlooked by Max Brod, who began to include them in his notes, notes which would someday become the basis of the biography that Brod would write about Franz Kafka.

At the university, Franz pored over his lawbooks. In April 1906 he took his examinations and, to his surprise, passed them. Immediately thereafter he was assigned to a Prague lawyer for a two-month period as an unpaid apprentice, a custom that went back to medieval times.

In that modern office, however, disillusionment was soon to descend, for as Franz accompanied the lawyer to court and heard actual cases being tried he could not help seeing that his beloved "justice" was hardly at issue, that it was usually a matter of the client's ability to afford a better representative to speak for him than his opponent could, and the outcome of a trial often depended on the cleverness of the lawyers in finding loopholes in the law. Moreover, he was told by the professionals around him, that he was naive to expect "pure justice" in a Prague or any other court. To a man such as Franz, whose mind constantly reached for a level of purity and rightness, this cynical attitude was almost intolerable. And yet he had committed himself to making the law his life's work.

In late June of that year Franz received his degree: Doctorate at Law. Putting off the thought of going into practice as long as possible, he got on a train and left the capital city to visit an uncle, Siegfried Löwy, a country doctor in Trest. From the worldly, sophisticated atmosphere of the courtroom Franz found himself in a mountain village, close to nature. Jogging along behind the doctor's horse through farmlands and forests, paying calls on the sick—rough-speaking peasants who looked up to the doctor as a god, or a scapegoat to blame for their ills—Franz realized his longing for a simpler life and felt himself responding to the elements: a storm in the mountains; the peace and beauty of a flowering sunlit valley; the human conditions of illness, of fear and death. The dry dissertations of his lawbooks were replaced by a flood of impressions that he registered with a kind of quiet excitement, knowing they were material for future stories.

One such experience was especially memorable, although not without some danger. It brought to mind the song, the ditty that Franz had chanted in childhood: "Be cheerful, the doctor's laid in bed, in the grave, beside you." That day, his uncle had paid a call on a man whose feverish face and labored breathing showed him to be in the last stages of pneumonia. His uncle could do little else for the patient but sponge his forehead with a cloth wrung out in cool water, and keep a vigil that went on into the evening, when the man died. The family that had gathered around the bed maintained a stony silence and glared at the doctor and his nephew; their expressions were vengeful, as if they thought the doctor had purposely withheld his healing powers because they could pay so little. It was with a great sense of relief that Franz climbed after his uncle into the horse-drawn cart and the two of them drove away, unharmed.

That evening, sitting up in the spare bed in his uncle's house, Franz began on a story that he called "A Country Doctor," in which the doctor, unable to cure his patient, climbs into the deathbed with him to share his fate—and the patient is not in the least grateful. What Franz did here, as he was often to do in later efforts, was to take a fanciful saying which reflected a true element of human nature, and treat it realistically; in so doing he plumbed to a deeper level of truth than, with few exceptions, had ever been reached in the form of fiction before.

Besides finding material for stories during his stay in the country, Franz found enjoyment in learning the rudiments of carpentry from a neighbor of his uncle's. On sunny mornings he could be found in the carpenter's backyard, hammering, sawing, and planing wood to make a table, two or three chairs, and a workbench. To do manual work, with hands that were large and very strong for such a slender man—he found to be especially satisfying, perhaps because before this he had only used his hands to write stories or do his lessons on history, dead languages, and the sawdust statements of the law.

This work was different, a healing experience, in which his hands felt the solid, warm surface of smooth wood, carved into it, shaped it, and made something different of it that was at once creative, beautiful, and useful.

October: and Franz, back in Prague and expected to take up his lifetime duties as a lawyer, was first assigned to the criminal court, a few months later to the civil. Until the following October (1907) he labored to prepare briefs, to represent clients fairly whether they could pay or not. At the end of the year he was obliged to acknowledge to himself that he was not nearly so clever as most of the other lawyers who opposed him. And the decisions being handed down by the judges often seemed to have little to do with justice. All this time his whole being was taken up with the desire to escape from the noisy, argumentative courtroom. A man could not set down a story if he was not permitted to pursue one quiet, reasonable, or imaginative thought.

If only he could get away from the law courts for even a few months, to flee the city and wander around the countryside by himself, have the time and peace to work out his ideas. It would not take much money, Franz reasoned; and in his desperation he dared consider asking his father for a little. The warehouse business, so Herrmann

Kafka had asserted with pride, had been doing very well recently. Thus one evening at the dining room table, Franz hesitantly broached the subject of a respite, a temporary freedom, from his practice of law.

At once Herrmann Kafka's mood, which had been expansive and jovial, turned truculent; and the next moment he launched into a tirade. What a miserable childhood *he* had had compared to the privileged treatment he had given his son and daughters: nothing, not a penny had ever been handed him on a silver platter! Franz listened numbly to the events of Herrmann Kafka's early struggles in life, the details of which he could have recited by heart.

After the tirade Franz rose from the table, pale and unable to touch his food, excused himself politely, and went to his room, where he lay for the next few hours in darkness, thinking of a way around his dilemma. Finally, in a half-asleep state bordering on nightmare, he began to weave a story, the first actual story that came to grips with a man, his thoughts, desires, and adventures. He called it "Wedding Preparations in the Country," and gave his male character the name of Raban, or "Raven," a name close to the crow, or jackdaw, of "Kafka." This Raban is obliged to go on a journey about which he feels reluctance and fear. Couldn't he do it the way he always did as a child in dangerous situations? He need not go himself, he would send his clothed body! Oh, this would be easy; as he lay in bed he would assume the shape of a huge beetle, then he would pretend that he was hibernating, and so of course could not get out of bed. He would whisper a few words of instruction to his body, which stood close to him, listening attentively. Then the body would bow obediently and go off to do his bidding, while he (impossible to move, of course, as a hibernating beetle) stayed in bed, confident that his "other" body would manage everything efficiently while he was at rest.

Thus, Franz imagined himself as two people, one of whom could be sent off airily to do the world's work, while the "real" Franz was free to lie in bed and day-dream.

After he had awakened from a short sleep and written this down, Franz experienced a sense of relief so complete and delightful that he was overwhelmed by it. He had discovered, perhaps on a mostly subconscious level, that by inventing another man whose name and personality were similar to his own, and then by giving this character *his* problems, the problems seemed to be transferred to this "other" man. It was a sort of protective measure, similar to the one in which a person, faced with an almost unbearable situation, such as the death of a loved one, will "stand back" and view his own actions as if they were those of another.

Because of the rebuffs and failures of his early life at home and in school, Franz had felt that his mind, in self-protection against further damage to its ego, had turned into what he called "a frozen sea." But Franz had not been happy with that concept, and he had sought, as he put it, for "an ax" to break into this dark, frigid sea so that its waters might flow with the energies of life.

In his writing, Franz Kafka found the ax to break the frozen sea.

Five

FRANZ SET FORTH from his family's apartment on a morning in 1907 to look for a job. He strode across the square dressed in the correct, sober uniform of a dark blue business suit, but he felt rather jaunty about the step he was taking. A job would mean meeting other people, no doubt many different types, and was that not what a writer needed for material? To be a hermit, as was Franz's natural inclination, was surely to turn one's back on life.

He was soon offered a position which would have meant having to appear in court and defend his clients volubly before judges and juries; this, he knew, he would be unable to do. And so he settled for an office job offered for only a year's duration, a condition which Franz felt to be an advantage. It was with an Italian insurance company with a branch in Prague. At first Franz applied himself with energy to the work, which consisted primarily of writing form letters. These letters required concentration on details—names, dates, and circumstances; the hours at his desk were long, boring, and confining, the pay was low, and all the time Franz's fertile mind was coming up with new, exciting ideas for stories he had no time to write down. In a matter of weeks he was feeling again the same sense of frustration he'd had when poring over his lawbooks.

After one such dreary day at the office, and with the specter of the next day looming before him, Franz sat at the little table in his room, with its two piles of books, a half-finished cup of coffee, and a pad of blank paper before him—and realized that his mind was too dulled, too dazed with boredom to remember any of the fresh, original ideas of a few hours before. But then he noticed something that he found to be a small, poignant sign that perhaps his body had ceased to be a stranger. His left hand was clasping his writing hand as if in sympathy!

In about a year the job came to an end; again he hoped for a breathing spell so he could go off somewhere and write, but his father had another idea. If Franz didn't want to work as a lawyer, why not come into the warehouse business with him? Franz was more dismayed at the thought of working there than of looking for another job.

He wrote to an uncle who had been one of the few pleasant memories of his childhood; Alfred was a lighthearted bachelor who had gone abroad to be general manager of the Spanish railways. He also wrote to another uncle who had left Prague for the Belgium Congo to take charge of a trading station, fitting out caravans. It seemed to Franz that either working with the railways in colorful Spain or helping outfit caravans in the wilds of Africa would be wonderfully superior to a routine job in a city office.

There is no record that either uncle ever answered.

Franz began listlessly walking the streets in search of another job, and writing at home, sometimes all through the night. In a long story he called "Description of a Struggle," he laid bare his own beginning longings for the companionship of women, who, so far, he hadn't admitted to his private world.

In "Struggle," one finds the self-mockery that was to become Kafka's trademark. A character known only as "the supplicant," but who is probably Franz himself, tries to make an impression on a young woman, but as he bows to her he finds to his embarrassment that his kneecap has been thrown out of joint. The girl adds to his unease by pointing out that she can actually see right through him, because he is made of yellow tissue paper, and so she shouldn't be annoyed by his actions, since he can't help bending to every breeze that comes into the room. (It would seem that Kafka was saying not only "If I try to win a girl, I'll certainly make a fool of myself," but also "She will see right through me, and know that I'll probably be fickle, and be swayed by the next pretty girl I set eyes on.") In the same story Franz adds to the self-mockery theme another one that he was to use often thereafter, that of, in effect, splitting the "real" Franz into two similar characters so that they can argue the pros and cons of a situation. Here the first man says he is engaged to a beautiful girl but is afraid of the turmoil in his mind at the thought of marriage. The second man is not at all sympathetic, and suggests that the only solution to the problem is to kill oneself. The first man thereupon pulls a knife out of his pocket and plunges it into his own arm. Horrified at the ensuing spurt of blood the second man claps a handkerchief over the wound; then he tries to cheer up his suicidal friend by pointing out how fortunate he is: he has a fine position and loyal friends, and when he and his bride ride off in their carriage there'll be singing and dancing in the streets. Despite these encouragements the other man gazes around in fright and distraction; none of this will help the situation or make him happy. Yet the author ends the scene on a rather optimistic note by having the depressed character say that perhaps he will think of something better in the morning.

The only bright spots in this period of Franz's life were his meetings with friends, especially Max Brod. Max was plodding along as a law clerk in the Prague post office and confessed to Franz that he really aspired to be a writer; in fact, he had already published a few articles in the local papers. At this revelation of Max's secret ambition, the floodgates of Franz's reserve broke down and he admitted that he had done some writing himself. Would Max perhaps mind listening to one or two of his amateur efforts?

Max listened, with surprise and gratification. It was almost immediately evident to him that here was real talent,

already shaped and sinewy, with an individual way of ex-
pressing ideas and images. At the end of the reading he
jumped to his feet declaring that such a story deserved to
be read by others.

Franz shrugged off the idea of getting himself published. He said he had entered a story in a contest two
years ago, in 1906, but that it hadn't even been given a
mention in the competition. And, to get to the truth of the
matter, he had such a high opinion of literature that he
did not think himself worthy to be called a writer. Max
insisted on seeing some more of his friend's work; Franz
obliged in the most self-deprecating manner, pointing out
every high-blown description and flowery phrase that he
said had to be pared away.

Max insisted that his friend submit two or three stories
for publication, but Franz stubbornly refused. Still, con-
fessing his ardent love of writing was a breakthrough for
Franz, and that day the two young men took a long walk
around the Old Town section of Prague, Franz pointing
out places he had found that were hidden from the busy
broad streets, places which had inspired his stories. They
strolled through narrow, twisted, cobbled lanes where
stone houses had been leaning for five hundred years, and
through spacious courtyards on whose balconies people
lingered to gossip. Franz was alive with observations:
Look at that great-grandmother—how delightful it was to
chuck an old woman under the chin! Think about steps—
if they're not worn hollow by the footsteps of people
would they not consider themselves soulless wood? See
that saint's statuette in the window? How lighthearted and
safe one must feel, believing in a household god!

Max, whose writing talents lay mainly in the field of journalism, was delighted to be given these interesting new glimpses of his city and he began to plan an article on the courtyards, with their old-world quiet and charm in the midst of the bustling modern city.

The day after their walk, Max again brought up the subject of submitting Franz's stories for publication. Franz said that he just couldn't do it. For the moment Max let the matter rest. After all, in spite of having had a few articles published, Max didn't see himself as a professional writer any more than did Franz. But they were both agreed on one point—their need to write. And so Max quit his job at the post office to join Franz in the search for a fairly well paying job which would let them out of work at an early hour, so that they could get to their "real" work while their creative energies were strong and fresh.

Making the rounds of the Prague firms the two young men soon found that when they specified the kind of job they were seeking, they were met with immediate hostility. "You are a Jew, no?" was asked of Max and Franz. "Surely you realize that such positions are scarce and in great demand." The inference was plain. Such positions are naturally reserved for Christians.

But these rebuffs didn't deter Franz or Max. They persisted, until Max got himself accepted as a "stringer" reporter for a theatrical publication; and Franz, in July 1908, found a job with a similar early closing hour. At first he was overjoyed with his luck.

The building was an imposing edifice topped by an ornate dome and fronted by Grecian columns serving no architectural purpose; its title seemed fittingly important: The Workers' Accident Insurance Institution for the Kingdom of Bohemia in Prague. Franz's office was on the second floor, and he was told he would be sharing it with a man named Treml. Herr Treml had watery blue eyes that never quite met Franz's open gaze, a scowl which Franz was soon to realize was a permanent fixture; and according to Max Brod who loathed him on sight, "urine-colored hair." Treml wore an old-fashioned high stiff collar which made it difficult for him to turn his head when someone knocked at the door; he would call a curt, impatient "Come in!" whereas Franz's own response in that office would always be a courteous "Please?" This Treml, a brusque and argumentative fellow, was to be Kafka's partner in that room for years to come.

Within the first few weeks Franz knew that his position as a law clerk in this insurance company, despite the early closing time, was going to prove just as frustrating as his former temporary job.

He would emerge from the building in midafternoon, in his familiar exhausted state of boredom after seven hours of bureaucratic paper work. The next hour would be spent walking about the city to clear his mind and for the exercise. Some days he would meet Max and they would spend an hour in a café, drinking coffee and discussing their latest writing projects. Then Franz would go home to sleep for a couple of hours. Next came dinner; and finally he would feel refreshed enough to turn to his writing. But unlike Max, with his short articles on various aspects of Prague and theatrical events which he was working on at the time, Franz's projects were far more ambitious. It was several hours before his imagination was at its freest, and its outpouring took most of the night and drained both mind and body. After sunrise Franz would get an hour or two of sleep and then it was time to go off to work again. Even the early closing hour was not going to solve the problem facing him: how to earn his living yet find enough time for his real life's work.

· And this was probably the reason why Franz did not quit and look for another job. For there could be no other job which would leave him any more time and energy for his writing.

But the picture was far from bleak. There was the company of Max Brod and other friends. In the next three years Franz took short holiday trips and summer vacations with Max, often accompanied by Max's brother Otto and the blind Oskar Baum. Franz enjoyed Oskar's ability to use his other senses more keenly than anyone with sight. They must be on a recently tarred road, with its wonderful smell; a hidden stream could be heard beyond the woods; it was going to rain in a few minutes but it wouldn't last long! The small group hiked all day in the mountains, swam in rivers and brooks, and performed stunts of daring on the mill weirs, diving over the short falls into the churning waters of the millrace. But Franz outdid the others when it came to maneuvering their canoe, or "man-drowner." While the others watched in apprehension from shore he would shoot the river's rapids lying down in the canoe, not even bothering to steer. "Suicidal" was the consensus beneath their cries of "Bravo!" as the little boat and its nonchalant passenger swirled safely at the bottom of the falls. Then Franz's face appeared, tanned and laughing, the picture of youth and health.

But often toward the end of these short periods away from the office he would suffer a severe bout of constipation, which, viewed in relation to his later illnesses, was very likely of a psychosomatic nature, an attempt of his body to render itself incapable of returning to work.

Since he had started working at the insurance company Franz had not shown Max any new writing. Max could see, to his frustration, that Franz was as far away as ever from allowing any of his stories to be submitted for publication. He knew that Franz had a mild contempt for anything to do with journalism for he was forever urging him to get on with the books he wanted to write. According to Franz, one wrote an article for the daily paper; the next morning it was used to wrap up garbage, and most such articles deserved this fate. Now, Max thought, if he could hit upon an idea for an article and persuade Franz to dash it off, he might not think of it as literature and would permit it to be published. Anything to get Franz over his stubborn block about submitting his private efforts to the harsh glare of the public. That block, Max suspected, may well have been based on Franz's extremely high regard for literature, but also on his fear of having his efforts rejected.

The idea for an article that Franz might be persuaded to write came about when Max heard about an airplane meet that was being held in the town of Brescia. Brescia was crowded for the occasion, as this was the world's first such gathering. Franz and Max, Otto and Oskar, with their limited funds, could find no better accommodations than a small room over a bar. A large hole had been cut in the center of the floor; the young men squatted down and peered at the noisy scene below; the barroom was crowded with some very tough-looking characters, and the four friends had the feeling that a robber, maybe even a cutthroat, would come up to relieve them of their money when they were asleep. Therefore they decided they would sleep in shifts to be on guard. But sleep was nearly impossible because of an ominous shrill noise that seemed to be coming from all around the building, and went on for hours. In the morning they were told the noise came from crickets, and the fact that they hadn't recognized the sound showed they were all "city stupids!" The next night in another town sleep was just as impossible, for this time they elected to stay in the anteroom of an ancient church, where hundreds of pictures of saints were stored, and they were forced to flee the room because of the bugs that scurried out from the frames. They sat up for the rest of the night on benches by the lake, shivering and trying to find some humor in their predicament.

But a good night's sleep wasn't half as important to Max as getting Franz to write about the airplane meet. Having let Otto and Oskar in on the plan, Max proposed to Franz that the four of them write their individual impressions of the event, and see whose turned out the best. Franz responded with enthusiasm, regarding the project as a lark. As soon as the four of them returned to Prague, Max Brod took Franz's version, which he honestly considered the best, to his newspaper publisher. The publisher scowled at the few pages, began penciling out line after line, and finally offered Max an almost insultingly small sum for the piece. Max accepted with alacrity.

Next week Max brought Franz Kafka his first published writing and waited anxiously for his friend's reaction. Franz looked at the page in surprise, then his face broke into a delighted smile. It was good, he admitted, to see his own name in print, even on a piece of journalism!

Encouraged, Max next came up with another idea based on their travels, a new type of guidebook to be called "Traveling Cheap." It was to include such categories as where to go for free concerts, how to live off the fruits of the countryside, what to do on rainy days, where not to stay (for instance, in old churches with bug-infested pictures of saints), and a section devoted to teaching the reader a foreign language quickly and "badly," because he was not going to learn it any other way in a short time. Franz took to this project with even more enthusiasm than the previous one; neither he nor Max had any facility with foreign languages, and Franz thought it delightful that they would be passing on their ignorance, their stumbling efforts, to others. To Max's gratification Franz contributed more and more items that showed him at his most witty and playful, such as a list of beaches where, in the considered opinion of the authors, the best-looking girls might be found.

Max took the idea of "Traveling Cheap" to several publishers around Prague, but each one wanted to know all their hard-won secrets before advancing a penny in payment, so nothing came of the venture except that it had kept Franz Kafka writing. But an editor of one of these publishing firms, seeing Kafka's name, remembered having read his article on the airplane meet and asked if Herr Kafka might have written anything else. This editor represented one of the most "literary" of the Prague journals. That day, Max was waiting for Franz in great excitement when he came out of work.

Right away Franz started to protest. The stories weren't "true" enough in what they were trying to say; they were full of windy rhetoric and needed to be trimmed to the bone. Max expostulated. Why, most of these disputed stories had already been trimmed down to an average of a page in length; any further trimming and they would disappear altogether! Still arguing, the two young men proceeded to Franz's house, where Franz ran to get his dictionary, complaining that he couldn't even spell well enough to deserve publication. Max, however, was adamant, and wouldn't leave until Franz had handed over half a dozen examples of his work.

The editor accepted the stories and printed them under the general title of "Contemplations." Max was jubilant; it seemed to him a sign that perhaps Franz could someday afford to quit his despised job and realize his dream of devoting his fresh, daytime energies to writing stories and books. Franz, of course, was happy to see his words in one of Prague's better journals; but he was afraid of having his hopes aroused. Resigned to his fate, that of a man with no money other than his modest weekly salary, he could get up every morning and go to the office; but if the spark of hope were kindled, then it seemed to him that every day would be a separate torment to endure. It was not unlike the state of mind of a man sentenced to life imprisonment without parole, and then parole is held out, only to be denied again and again. And in the end, he felt, any hopes that he might dare to entertain would surely be extinguished.

Some readers would scorn such an attitude and call it defeatist. But Kafka, in his own knowledge of the world, was only being realistic. Of all the writers he had ever heard of, there were less than half a dozen who had been able to earn a living solely with their pens. A man had to be practically as famous and as prolific, say, as his favorite author, Charles Dickens, whom he read in German translation, before he could afford to sit at his desk all day and write fiction. Even the great Honoré de Balzac had spent most of his life half-starving and hounded by debt collectors.

The immediate fate of the stories called "Contemplations" was that by the time the journal had brought out its next issue they had been virtually forgotten—no reviews, no critic's voice raised in either praise or condemnation. Franz had expected nothing better; but he was grateful to Max for his efforts. And although Franz's attitude was one of resignation, his reactions were spirited and human enough when, a few months later, after having a few prose poems published, a critic wrote that he didn't understand what this "F. Kafka" was trying to say. Franz exclaimed, striking the offending review with the flat of his hand, that the critic was obviously an idiot, as he, Kafka, had gone to great lengths to state some small truth of life in the plainest possible way.

And so, despite the acceptance of his few creative efforts, Franz stayed on at the insurance company, and was even beginning to use his observations of the people he met on the job as future material. In fact, so multitudinous were his impressions that in 1910 he began to keep a diary, which he was to continue up to the year before his death. He realized that his dull paperwork translated itself into the flesh-and-blood needs and demands of workers insured by the company, men who came into his office in the course of trying to collect insurance for injuries or illness and were confronted by Franz, Herr Treml, or their superiors. Why should these hard-working people be forced into the ignominious position of begging for what was rightfully theirs? They should rise in righteous wrath, storm the Institution, and smash it to smithereens. Many of these impassioned sentiments were delivered by Franz to Max when they met after work on the corner. One can picture the confirmed pacifist, Franz Kafka, dressed in his well-pressed dark suit, hair carefully combed and shoes shined, shaking his fist at the monolithic mass of bureaucracy. A figure of humanitarian passions, forever frustrated in action.

And in that same year, 1910, there was another frustration in Franz's life—in his need for the company of women. He confessed to Max that he had a kind of crush on one of the actresses of the Yiddish Theatre Troupe that was playing in Prague. He regarded the woman from a reverent distance and regretted that soon she would be leaving town with the company. Another day Franz told his friend he had met a prostitute on the street and gone with her to her room. She had been lonely, he said, but had given him no real comfort, and so he had given her none.

In both cases these were women with whom Franz

could hardly have formed a lasting relationship. From the beginning, Franz Kafka was setting a pattern that thereafter he was to labor mightily to break.

Six

THE YEAR 1911 began for Franz on a note of healthful activity, a trip away from the city. But by the end of the year he was considering suicide.

A business trip took Franz to many small towns in the Czech countryside, and what he enjoyed most was the time spent on trains. There he was free to daydream and to write, with nobody to interrupt him with phone calls and no unhappy workers coming in to ask him to plead their case with the insurance company; and all the while he was getting paid by the company.

In the summer Franz and Max managed to get to Milan in northern Italy, where they enjoyed opera from the top and cheapest seats, nearly parallel with the chandeliers; and to Paris, where they climbed the parapets of famous churches and admired their hideously grinning or musing gargoyles, reminiscent of those on the ancient Prague churches. On their way home Franz came down with his predictable case of constipation, this time augmented by a more serious illness, a bad cold that caused some difficulty in breathing. After suffering for several weeks he gave in to Max's persuasion and took leave from the insurance office to go to a health resort in the mountains. He returned to Prague feeling cured, and full of enthusiasm over the "completely natural life" the people in charge had advised: no medicines, let nature work its wonders, dress lightly, sleep with the windows open, even in winter, drink no alcohol, and be a vegetarian. No more meat or fish! Franz, with childhood memories of having to keep up with his father's gargantuan appetite, was relieved to say good-bye to the consumption of meat and fish. On a visit to a local aquarium he gaily greeted the fish swimming around in their tanks; now he could enjoy looking at them since he wouldn't be eating them anymore.

He had also become a member of a literary group. The well-to-do, if fairly small, set of Prague's Jewish society was headed by a brilliant woman, Berta Franta. Madame Franta gathered about herself for good conversation such young men as Max Brod and Franz Werfel—the latter to write many books, including *The Song of Bernadette;* and Albert Einstein, a young Swiss-German professor at the Prague University. Franz found the talk exhilarating, although Professor Einstein didn't interest him much at first. Thick black hair springing from his forehead like a brush, Einstein stood before his little group of listeners and sketched on the backs of envelopes the wonders of a thing he called "an atom." This atom, the smallest conceivable particle of matter, said Einstein, contained in its "nucleus" hundreds of thousands of volts of energy, although, he added, as a theoretical physicist he doubted if this energy could ever be released.

But then Einstein began talking about "nationalism" and Franz's attention picked up. The young professor spoke with fervor of the similarity of his own growing up in two countries to the situation he had found in the Czech-German-Jewish city of Prague. He would never forget the "open hatred" his classmates in school had shown toward the students of a neighborhood school. "Numerous fights took place, with many a battered head resulting." At this, several members of the literary group glanced at Oskar Baum, the victim of just such a street fight. Nationalism, yes, even patriotism, continued Einstein, brought out the worst in human beings, setting those who called themselves citizens of one country against those of all other countries. "Patriotism is a shrine that a man keeps in his house," said the young professor, "and it holds the moral requisites of animal hatred and mass murder that, in case of war, he obediently takes out for his service. . . . Instead of such a shrine it would be better if you had in your room a piano, or a bookcase!" Einstein ended by declaring, "The state, to which I belong as a citizen, does not play the least role in my spiritual life; I regard allegiance to a government as a business matter, somewhat like the relationship with a life insurance company."

Franz Kafka listened to the words of this impassioned young professor and could hardly believe his ears. For here were his own exact beliefs, which up to then he had never ventured to voice. In that time and place, the Prague of 1912, the Czech people were in a state of near-revolution, so great was their longing for a country of their own, a "Czech-oslovakia." But Franz Kafka, Czech-German-Jew, had never been given the concept of a country to which he might conceivably belong. Now, the words of Albert Einstein affected him in a positive, almost joyous, manner. Patriotism, he had said, set the citizens of one country against those of all other countries; therefore, if a man was *not* a citizen of any country he might belong to all countries! Einstein's convictions appealed to Franz as a writer; his curiosity about the citizens and customs of all places would have already placed him outside the narrow confines of nationalism even if the circumstances of his birth had not done so. But it was good to hear his own secret and unpopular convictions expressed openly by such an authority as a university professor.

In the cafés that Franz and his friends frequented there were likely to be Czech anarchists at the next table, openly plotting the overthrow of the Austro-Hungarian monarchy. But at Franz's table nobody was plotting anything more momentous than how to get away from work in time to see the Yiddish Theatre Troupe, which was again in town. Franz had got over his crush on the lovely actress he'd worshipped from a distance, but had befriended one of the young actors, named Isaac Löwy (no close relative to his mother). Löwy was a childlike innocent whose specialty was playing the clown; Franz teased him about his gentle manners when, after all, his name meant "lion." Feeling that Löwy needed the warmth of a family around him Franz invited Isaac to his house. After his visit, Herrmann Kafka spat out his opinion in the form of a familiar German proverb: "If you lie down with dogs you will get up with fleas." Franz knew that his father disapproved of the young man as he disapproved of most of his son's friends, simply because they were his friends. And he felt that the sensitive Löwy had been treated without hospitality in the Kafka house. Therefore Franz went out of his way to be kind to Löwy, who was having problems with his job, his love life, and his health, none of which Franz could do anything about; but when Löwy and his troupe left Prague, Franz followed him with letters in which there was concern but not a shred of pity. He, Franz, was not giving up hope for Löwy; he despaired easily but he was easily made happy, a fact he should remember when in the depth of despair. And, above all, he should look after his health in preparation for better days.

His cheerful comforting of friends did not always serve in his own behalf. His work load at the insurance company was getting heavy because everybody had learned to turn to that most efficient and patient of clerks, F. Kafka, and there were days when his complaints to Max sounded far different from the times when he had railed against his bosses for not paying the workers' damage claims. If Max only knew how much he had to do! Franz went on to compare his responsibilities in a humorous manner that uncannily anticipated the still-to-come films of Charlie Chaplin. Accident claims were coming in at a tremendous rate, it seemed to Franz. People were falling off ladders into their own machinery, breaking their legs by tripping over boards, and putting up equipment that promptly fell on their heads; and as for all those young women working in china factories who insisted on hurling themselves down flights of stairs amid torrents of crockery—they were positively giving him a headache!

But the following week gave Franz a worse headache. Somebody at the office had seen some of his drawings, sketches of the stick figures he was always making and then tossing into the wastebasket. And the official who'd fished those drawings out of Franz's basket had deemed them so good that he had appointed Franz "drafting clerk," along with his other duties. Franz and several other new drafting clerks had been summoned before a high official of the company. In a state of apprehension over being assigned additional boring duties, Franz listened to the official, who had launched into a speech. To Franz's surprise the speech was not on the nature of the new duties but on the signal honor that had just been bestowed, and how he was confident in their ability to add further luster to the name and prestige of the company in performing these duties in a manner that would distinguish them, modest as was their position, in the eyes of their superiors. At this point Franz suddenly burst out laughing, and despite the shocked expression on the speaker's face he couldn't stop.

Now he was afraid of losing his job, the job that, dull as it was, at least left him free in midafternoon. He sought out Max Brod in apprehension. Max helped him draft a letter of apology to the high official. Fortunately the man was not without a sense of humor, and after admitting he had been a bit pompous, he assured Franz that he was a valued employee.

And then still another element entered the picture, which threatened to rob Franz of the rest of the hours left to his day. His father had fallen ill; the works manager of his office-warehouse was away on business; and now Herrmann Kafka wanted Franz to go to the warehouse, when he was through at the office, and watch the men to be sure they didn't steal any merchandise or lie down on the job. The elder Kafka had made this request while lying in his bed in the daytime, an unheard-of state of affairs; he muttered something about its being the least an only son could do while he was still living under his parents' roof. When Franz did not immediately respond with "All right, Father," Herrmann Kafka turned his head wearily to the wall.

Next, his mother was whispering to him about how unhappy his father would be if Franz refused to help. After all, she pointed out, he was free in the middle of the afternoon, and had nothing to do with the rest of his day except to scribble away at *stories!*

Franz had long since realized that his mother and father had not the slightest idea of how important his "scribbling" was to him; but since *he* knew how important it was, he put off his answer for a day or two. To Franz, his father's request assumed the proportions of a cruel dilemma. It was unthinkable to refuse his father, when he was still trying to win his love and respect. But it was equally unthinkable to give in and take on the added duties, which would prevent him from having any time at all to write, and life would be quite intolerable. And there were other reasons for Franz's shrinking from taking on the extra work, reasons which he himself probably did not consciously understand. One was, that in appearing at his father's office in the role of overseer Franz would be, in effect, taking his father's place. This was a part that Franz was to be unable to play, at that time or any future time in his life. Added to this was the fact that he would be not only acting the part of his father, but his father as a villain, feared and detested by his employees because of his overbearing treatment of them—and Franz was still denying this facet of his father's character, still trying to cast him in a heroic role. The situation was further complicated by Franz's fear that, even if he tried to supervise the workers and watch for such lapses as their petty thievery, he would probably not catch these acts, and when his father returned to work he would discover the missing items and upbraid his son for his inability to take his place, even temporarily. All these fears and alarms, however half-buried in his subconscious, nevertheless came to the surface shortly thereafter in his writing, disguised by fictional names and inverted situations, the only way Franz Kafka could allow himself any emotional release.

Consciously he was certain of just one thing—that if he agreed to go to the warehouse he would be condemning himself to an unknown stretch of dull gray working days in which there would not be one hour in the twenty-four when he could hope to get any good writing done. The next day, when Franz met Max outside the office, he was in a state of extreme agitation: his words spilled out and his hands flew about in violent gestures. He said he had just spent the last two days working on a long, pompous speech for one of the officials to give, and it had been like tearing a piece of flesh out of his own body to waste all that time writing "sawdust" when he'd been burning with inspiration for a new story, and now— And now! Franz burst out with the news of his father's request. Max heard it for what it was, an inchoate cry of despair.

Max was beside himself; he told Franz that he was an idiot if he let his family do this to him. A creative artist had to be selfish or else the world would move in and leave him not one moment to himself. Franz didn't answer, but strode ahead, hands in pockets, gazing at the ground. Max thought of the example of another artist, the great musician Mozart, whose father did not see why his son could not use a part of the day after he was through composing, earning some money by teaching pupils to play the pianoforte. Mozart had refused, courteously but firmly, explaining that he needed several hours a day to rest after his intense creative activity. And Max added that Mozart's father had taken no for an answer.

Max's arguments were to no avail. Franz could not refuse his father's call for assistance. The next day he reported for work at the warehouse.

For the next few days he stayed up most of every night to write, going directly to work at the insurance company the next morning. But inevitably there came a night when he fell into bed, unable to sit up at his table. And then it seemed to him as if the characters in his brain had somehow broken loose and were beating wildly against his rib cage. His breath became labored; he could hear the hammering of his heart; and lying there alone in the darkness he kept murmuring over and over to himself, "It *can't* be good for you. . . ."

One day about two weeks later, Franz met Max after an absence of several days, and to Max's surprise he seemed quite cheerful. Had Franz's father recovered and relieved him of his duties at the warehouse? No, was the reply, but Franz was in much better spirits that day than he had been recently. Last night, he said, again totally unable to work on his writing and with his head feeling as if it would burst, he had stood at his bedroom window and contemplated jumping out of it. As Max listened in growing horror Franz described how he had stood there for a long time, his forehead pressed to the pane of glass which could so easily be raised; and had considered rather absently how startled the toll-keeper on the nearby bridge would be at the sight of a body hurtling past him. And then, just as he had decided to jump, he had realized that he owed his friend Max a letter of farewell, and he didn't have the strength to write it. So, concluded Franz in his most lighthearted voice, he had walked back to his bed, reasoning that if he killed himself he would be interrupting his writing for an even longer time than at present!

Franz's cheerful rationality did not calm his friend's fears. Hastily, Max wrote a letter to Franz's mother, telling her that with no time in his day to work on what she might consider to be of no importance, but to her son was as important as air to breathe and water to drink, he was in grave danger of suicide.

The letter apparently brought Julie Kafka to her senses, for she responded promptly that she appreciated Max's concern and she would pretend to her sick husband that Franz was going to the warehouse every day, and meanwhile she would try to find somebody else to take his place.

At least Franz in his not too happy life was blessed with good and true male friends. And now to appear was the first important woman.

Seven

ON AUGUST 13, 1912, Franz wrote in his diary that at Max Brod's house he had met a certain "F.B." This use of initials to protect the identity of a woman with whom one was having, or planning to have, a more than casual relationship was already rather old-fashioned by Kafka's time but it was characteristic of his extreme sensitivity to a woman's right to her privacy and dignity.

When Franz first met "F.B." she was sitting at a table in Max Brod's apartment. Franz saw that she had dark brown hair, large dark eyes, and was not particularly good-looking; still, he was immediately attracted to her. Max introduced her as Felice Bauer, the manager of a large Berlin firm which had a branch in Prague, hence the reason for her visit. Franz had never before met a woman who was, as far he he could surmise, financially independent, and it is suggested that this was the point at which he became seriously interested in Fräulein Bauer. He saw her immediately as a possible wife who would work and bring home her share of the food and rent money. Up to that moment Franz could not imagine himself taking on the responsibility of a wife, reasoning that if he did not marry perhaps someday he might be able to quit his hated job and write for most of the day, but that with a wife he would never be able to do this.

Now, however, with the arrival of Felice Bauer, a successful young woman in business, Franz Kafka's ideas about marriage took an abrupt turn in a more optimistic direction. For the rest of her visit the lady from Berlin found herself almost exclusively in the company of the young man from Prague.

Franz felt that he was in love with Felice; and yet he let her return to Berlin without telling her. He still could not quite bear to propose marriage, with all the responsibility that such a step would bring with it. But meanwhile he was bursting with happiness and energy. Thanks to the intervention of Max Brod in seeking the assistance of Franz's mother, the warehouse job had been lifted from his shoulders. And his creative drive, stimulated by his new interest in a woman, surged to an unprecedented peak. On the night of September 22nd Franz sat at his work table from 10:00 P.M. to 6:00 A.M. without a break, and without the slightest sense of fatigue. The story that he was to call "The Judgment" (also to be known as "The Verdict") seemed to spurt up like a geyser; there was no hesitation about what to write next. The words raced along down page after page, sixteen pages in all, and it was done.

"The Judgment" was to be published in Kafka's lifetime—meeting with the usual lack of interest—but in the fifty years since its appearance, critics the world over have held it up as the turning point in Kafka's writing, the moment when he succeeded in breaking through to the form of fiction that was exactly suited to his genius.

As so often in Kafka's stories, the characters in "The Judgment" seem straightforward and ordinary to begin with, their problems familiar and everyday. And yet as one follows them along one is suddenly in another dimension in which people do not act as one would expect, events grow murky and threatening, until all is engulfed in a mist of horror. Much has been said about such stories of Kafka's, as for instance the writer-philosopher Albert Camus's summation: "His art consists in compelling us to reread him." Another quote comes to mind, in a mocking, dancing vein that seems well suited to Kafka's tone—a line from a Gilbert and Sullivan operetta: "Things are seldom as they seem!"

And so in "The Judgment" we have what at first seems a simple story about Georg, a young man who has become engaged to a "Frieda Brandenfeld," and he is wondering how best to break the news to his friend, a less fortunate fellow with no girl of his own. To seek advice about this he goes into his widowed father's room, a step he hasn't taken in months, and he is surprised to see how dark it is. His father is sitting at his window reading a newspaper, and Georg finds him a pitiful sight—old, weak, and toothless—and feeling that he ought to be in bed he lifts him and carries him over to the bed, then covers him with blankets. He then tells his father about his engagement and how he is hesitating about breaking the news to his friend. The father answers in a very strange way. First he denies that Georg *has* this friend; and next he asks if George thinks he is well covered up. Georg assures his father that he is indeed well covered up in the bed; but at this, the father throws off the blankets and "springs erect upon the bed." He declares that Georg has wanted him covered up forever but that Georg's dead mother has left him all her strength. Then with the utmost bitter triumph he claims that of course he knows Georg's friend, that "he would have been a son after my own heart," and that he has actually taken the friend away from Georg, and he is now *his* friend. Not only that, but if Georg dares to claim his bride, he, the father, will take her from him as well. The terrible tirade ends with the father condemning Georg as a devil of a human being, and sentencing him to death that very day, by drowning!

Georg rushes from the room as his father's body crashes down upon the bed. Then the young man runs down the street and jumps onto the nearby bridge, at the same time seeing himself as the renowned athlete he had been as a boy. As he swings over the side he murmurs in farewell to his father and mother that he has always loved them. At the moment he lets himself drop into the water below he has the impression of an unending stream of traffic rushing by on the bridge.

As in earlier stories, Franz has again used two versions of himself. The first is Georg, who has become engaged as Franz himself wished to be (to a Frieda Brandenfeld, "F.B.," or Felice Bauer). The other man is a lonely fellow who lives far away, cut off from most human contacts, just as that "half" of Franz wished he could be, a hermit free to weave his stories. Georg seeks out his father ostensibly to ask his advice on how to break the news to his friend; or is it to ask his advice as to whether he, Georg, should be contemplating marriage? Now, Franz Kafka's actual father was a powerful figure, despite his recent illness, whereas "Georg's" father is shown as being old and weak, as well as widowed, altogether a pitiable and impotent figure. But what happens when Georg, conscience-stricken at having neglected his father (for which we may substitute: not loved him) comes into the old man's room? The invalid is almost immediately transformed into a strong and virile figure who "springs erect upon the bed." It would seem that the author may have wished his father to be an old and helpless weakling, but in his heart he knew this was not so, and he could not preserve this image in the story. Georg's outraged father reproaches his son for wanting him to be "covered up," that is, covered with earth as in the grave. And then the father, in revenge, becomes superhumanly powerful; he boasts that he has already stolen his friend away—the friend whom his father loves as a son—and will even steal from him the woman he wants to marry.

Franz made the father in the story a widower, no doubt for the fictional purpose of having him "eligible"; but there is probably a deeper reason. In his diaries Franz wrote later that his mother's treatment of him as a child had left him without comfort. In another story, he has his Franz character say that mothers could be wonderful but that he lost his as a child. And so, in "The Judgment," Franz has shown to all intents and purposes a subconscious deathwish. He has already eliminated the mother, and although he elevates the father to his actual powers, he causes him to collapse just before he pronounces the death sentence on his son. It is as if Kafka were saying, "You have made it impossible for me to love you, try as I have, and therefore I wish you were both dead, and of course for this wish I too deserve to die."

And so, in the story, everyone dies after Georg has been judged unworthy of being a son and a future husband. Thereupon Georg accepts the sentence and drowns himself; but he cannot resist the chance to reproach his parents, reminding them (in such a poignant and boyish way) of how proud they had been of him as a gymnast, and of how he had always loved them in spite of the early death they had brought him to. And yet, for all its morbid mood, the story pulses with life. When Franz read his manuscript to Max Brod he went over that last scene in which, at the moment of Georg's suicide, he was conscious of an unending stream of traffic rushing by on the bridge. He admitted to Max that when he had written the end of the story he had had in mind the sensation of a violent sexual ejaculation.

"The Judgment" is worth the lengthy exploration it has been given here because it is filled with clues to Franz Kafka's personality. It is probable that falling in love for the first time in his life provided an emotional release that allowed him to admit his hitherto buried resentments, at least in the disguise of fiction. In "The Judgment," he himself was the judge, delivering the sentence of death to his parents and himself for their inability to love, and incidentally showing that his three sisters, so much younger than he, had no part in the terrible emotional tensions of the triangle of mother, father, and son. But "The Judgment" did even more: it gave notice, as it were, that Franz Kafka was far from convinced in his mind about entering into marriage. As he showed in the story, one part of himself longed to be a family man, but the other part longed to be alone, to dream, and to write.

He had not nearly enough time for writing now; what would life be like if he were obliged to share *all* his time with another person? Felice Bauer had already shown an almost total lack of interest and understanding of Franz's need to be alone, to create. And so he wrote to the girl he loved, in Berlin, and she answered, inviting him to come up for a visit. Franz replied with many expressions of his honest feelings, his deep affection, and not without a show of the charm he was always to bring to bear with women. It was real charm, the sort that reflects a true consideration for the other person, not a superficial desire to appear charming. But it was a substitute for action. And so Franz threw himself into a project, a long story called "The Stoker." It concerned a young man named Karl who had got a young woman pregnant, and his parents had urged him to escape marriage by boarding a ship bound for America. On board Karl soon makes friends with a stoker, a rough burly fellow whom Karl finds fine company. The friendship is broken up by Karl's uncle, an American of great importance, who calls the stoker ignorant, unworthy of being Karl's friend. In

America Karl is persuaded to take a job in a large hotel where he is miserable doing work that bores him; finally he rebels and dares hope for a bit of happiness by joining a traveling circus.

Here again, as in "The Judgment," one can see the events of Franz Kafka's own life, plus his fears and hopes, mirrored in the fictional events of his story. To begin with, the hero (or, as we would probably call him today, the "antihero") could certainly have been Kafka himself. He is called by a name beginning with K—Karl—and Kafka was to go on to call other leading characters in his stories Joseph K. and simply "K." At the time Kafka wrote this story he was involved in a physical relationship with Felice Bauer and he may well have been wondering what he would do if she became pregnant and, as a result, wanted him to marry her. One doesn't know what Franz Kafka would have done in reality, but in his story, "Karl" flees the country, with his parents' blessing. And this flight is to America, a place Kafka had longed for years to see. On the ocean voyage Karl makes friends with a man who earned his living at hard physical labor, a type much admired by Kafka, who was always to find himself more at ease in the company of men than women, since men did not represent any threat, any danger, to the peace of his private life. Next in the story, a man of great importance interferes to break up this friendship just as Herrmann Kafka had tried to break up the friendship between Franz and his friend Isaac Löwy, the little fellow of the traveling theatrical troupe. In America Karl is persuaded to conform to middle-class society and he takes a job in a large hotel establishment doing boring work (just as Kafka worked in the Accident Insurance Institution). Finally, in Kafka's wish fulfillment, he has Karl escape this tiresome occupation by joining a traveling circus—a happy escape from his own real life that Kafka could never actually dare to make.

"The Stoker" was to become the first chapter of a book that Kafka was never to finish, called *Amerika*. While he was writing it he would stroll along the streets of Prague in the evening, watching the people lighting the tall gas lamps outside their houses, lamps that an associate of Mr. Thomas Edison of America had recently installed. Franz would wander down cobbled alleys and through flowery courtyards, plotting his next scene and murmuring with a secret smile American Indian words that intrigued him with their mysterious syllables, such as "Ok-la-*ho*-ma, Ok-la-*ho*-ma." The concept of the American Indian that Franz had read about in stories appealed to him immensely. He wished, in one of his daydreams, that he might be an Indian on a fast horse, leaning against the wind, shedding his spurs, then throwing away the reins.

In another daydream he saw himself as a small boy waiting in the Jewish Town Hall with a hundred other people for their American visas. There was his father in the center, talking with other men; there was his mother, heavily wrapped and rummaging in the traveling bundles, and his sisters chattering with other girls. In a few weeks, he knew, they would all arrive in America. Of course it wouldn't be as simple as that, he realized, with his unfailing attention to logic; there'd be the misery of dysentery, and there were unsympathetic Christians shouting at them through the windows; and even quarrels among the Jews themselves—short, fierce but fairly harmless knife fights over some small argument. But, Franz felt, there would be enough boys like himself running around, climbing over the mattresses and waiting around for the bread that somebody was always spreading with something nourishing. And so he would get enough to eat, he would reach America, and all would be well.

The America of 1912 that Franz imagined, he was never to see. But the following year, through Max Brod's endeavors, the first part of the book, the story about the stoker, was published.

Franz sought out his friend Max, now happily married, and told him of his intense feelings for Felice Bauer and his desire to ask her to become his wife. He said fervently that marrying, accepting all the children that came, and supporting them in an insecure world and perhaps guiding them as a father, was the utmost a human being could succeed in accomplishing. Max assured Franz that he was as capable as any other man, and advised that he should ask Felice's hand in marriage.

But Max, as well as Franz, had his doubts. He knew the deep schism in Franz's personality, the two opposing tendencies that fought for supremacy: the longing for aloneness and the desire to be sociable. Max remembered an unpublished fragment of one of Franz's stories in which a character says that at one time he had a job with a small railroad in the heart of Russia. The wider the aloneness that surrounded him the better pleased he was. In another story, a character declares that the most wonderful, quiet, and idle experience in his life was the time when he had broken his leg and was obliged to give up all responsibilities, to lie around the house and have people attend to his wishes.

To wrestle with this biggest dilemma of his life so far, Franz again turned, as he had with carpentry, to working with his hands, this time with gardening, to which he donated his services, helping landscape a terrace in a beautiful suburban park outside Prague. Max sometimes went along on a weekend afternoon. Franz worked swiftly and expertly with a trowel, digging into the rich, sharp-scented earth, his back feeling the heat of the summer sun. To Max he looked for all the world as if he were working in his own garden; but Franz's thoughts were far from those of a contented householder, planting his own flowers and shrubs. "The responsibility," he kept repeating. He was haunted by the responsibility that a man took on for the life of another person, and the children that the union would no doubt produce.

Max himself, having accepted such responsibilities, said little in reply; he must have realized that Franz mainly wanted a listener. Often he would pause halfway through his chore of digging a hole for a plant, or pruning a bush, and he would attempt to convince Max that his reasons for putting off telling Felice Bauer his feelings and intentions were strong and valid. The main thing was the prospect of living in small quarters day after month after year, the dreaded as well as the longed for intimacy of marriage. And yet the moment after he had shaken his head over the futility of such a smothering way of life he was shuddering over the thought of its alternative, of leaving his parents' house eventually to live alone in some dreary furnished room, probably a series of them, and facing the twin assaults of old age and sleeplessness (in that order, as he put it). Franz usually ended these debates by assuring Max he would probably marry Felice if only to give himself the strength and inspiration to get through the rest of his natural life.

Despite his indecision Franz's creative energies were still fantastically high. In November 1912 came "The Metamorphosis," an enduring classic that begins with a sentence twice as chilling for the matter-of-fact way it is stated: "As Gregor Samsa awoke one morning from uneasy dreams he found himself transformed in his bed into a gigantic insect." The tale goes on to show Gregor, a young man—at least he had gone to bed the night before as such—saying to himself, as he lies there in his new loathsome condition, that he cannot believe it is real. Thereupon he rationalizes this sorry state by thinking of the exhausting job he has chosen, which entails his getting up so early that it makes him a dullard, stumbling to work half asleep; and if he didn't have to please his parents he'd have given notice long ago; but there was some hope—once he'd saved enough money he would quit the job, leave his parents, and become completely free.

Gregor, after rationalizing calmly that this metamorphosis of his body must be an illusion, finally realizes that it is real enough and he is unable to turn back into a human being. He leaves his room and sees the horrified reaction of his father to his inhuman appearance. His father seizes a walking stick and drives the huge bug that Gregor has become back into his room. For awhile Gregor's mother and sister try to accommodate and tol-

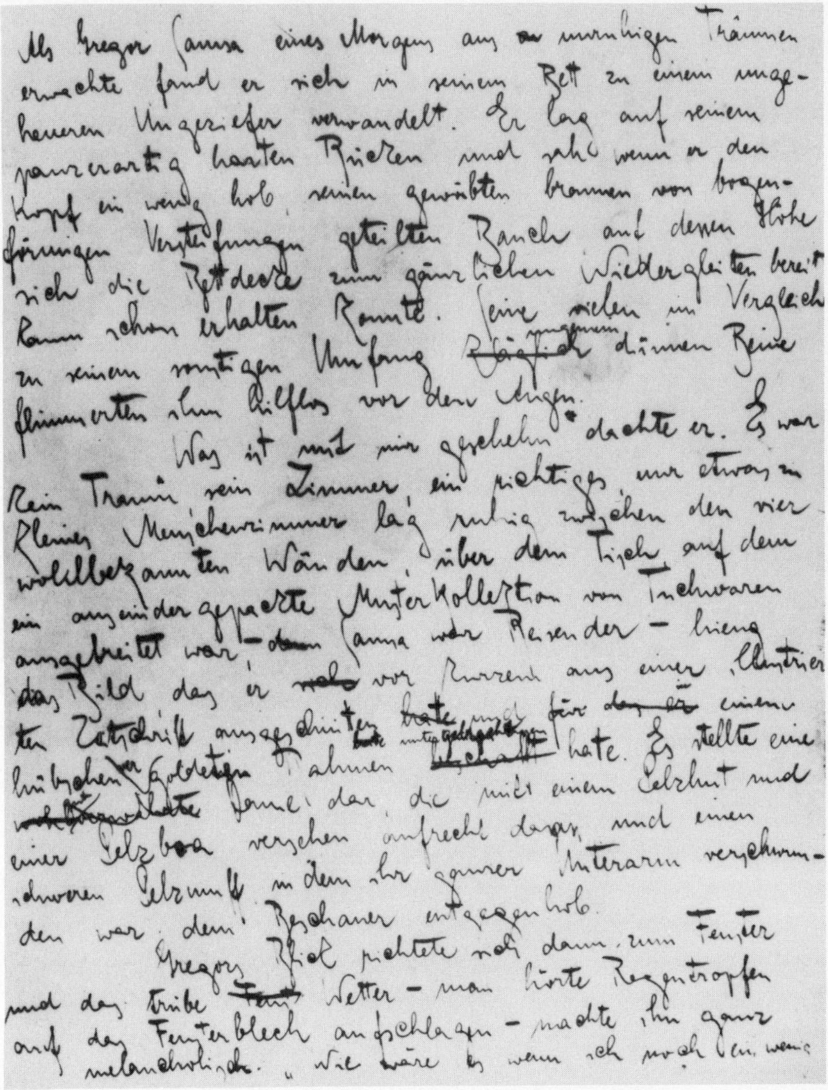

Als Gregor Samsa eines Morgens aus ~~a~~ unruhigen Träumen
erwachte fand er sich in seinem Bett zu einem unge-
heueren Ungeziefer verwandelt. Er lag auf seinem
panzerartig harten Rücken und sah wenn er den
Kopf ein wenig hob, seinen gewölbten braunen von bogen-
förmigen Versteifungen geteilten Bauch auf dessen Höhe
sich die Bettdecke zum gänzlichen Niedergleiten bereit
kaum schon erhalten konnte. Seine vielen im Vergleich
zu seinem sonstigen Umfang ~~kläglich~~ jämmerlich dünnen Beine
flimmerten ihm hilflos vor den Augen.
„Was ist mit mir geschehen" dachte er. Es war
kein Traum sein Zimmer ein richtiges nur etwas zu
kleines Menschenzimmer lag ruhig zwischen den vier
wohlbekannten Wänden, über dem Tisch auf dem
eine auseinandergepackte Musterkollektion von Tuchwaren
ausgebreitet war – ~~denn~~ Samsa war Reisender – hieng
das Bild das er ~~vor~~ vor kurzem aus einer illustrier-
ten Zeitschrift ausgeschnitten [illegible] und für [illegible] einen
hübschen vergoldeten Rahmen [illegible] hatte. Es stellte eine
[illegible] Dame dar, die mit einem Pelzhut und
einer Pelzboa versehen aufrecht dasass und einen
schweren Pelzmuff in dem ihr ganzer Unterarm verschwun-
den war, dem Beschauer entgegenhob.
Gregors Blick richtete sich dann zum Fenster
und das trübe ~~Fens~~ Wetter – man hörte Regentropfen
auf das Fensterblech aufschlagen – machte ihn ganz
melancholisch. „Wie wäre es wenn ich noch ein wenig

A portion of the first draft of "The Metamorphosis."

erate the creature, but the father is enraged by it, and one day hurls a dish of apples in its direction; one of these lodges in the insect's back, causing an infection; Gregor drags himself around the room for awhile and then dies, his last thoughts loving ones of his family.

Franz Kafka had written earlier, in 1906, of turning into an insect in order to let his body go off on an unwanted journey while his mind stayed peacefully at home; and in "The Judgment" his father had passed a sentence of death on him. Here the two themes were joined into one even more terrible: My father regards me as nothing better than an insect and kills me himself.

Regardless of the psychological implications, the literary evidence was, in Max Brod's opinion, superb; he called it a glorious story even though it was about a noxious insect. ("The Metamorphosis" was published three years later. Franz showed part of his gratitude to Max by dedicating the hard-cover edition of his short stories, now called, without an "s," *Contemplation,* which came out in 1913, to "M.B." In 1972 "The Metamorphosis" and "The Judgment" were put on as legitimate plays in New York theatres.)

At the end of the year Franz could no longer stand his own procrastination and Felice's loving, questioning letters. His first step toward becoming engaged, however, was not to ask Felice but to seek out his father.

He told Herrmann Kafka that he was thinking of being betrothed. His approach was that of a son needing his father's permission, his blessing for getting himself engaged to be married when he was a grown man of twenty-nine.

Or was it, perhaps, that Franz subconsciously hoped that his father would try to talk him out of this important step, in effect forbidding it by pointing out all the troubles he himself had taken on by marrying and assuming the responsibilities of head of a family? Something of this nature seems likely, and perhaps Herrmann Kafka sensed the role that Franz was trying to get him to play, for his reply showed that he wanted no part in Franz's decision. The elder Kafka simply gave a growl of anger followed by a few harsh words to the effect that Franz was long since of age and that he, his father, had no advice to give him.

There was, then, nothing else for Franz to do but to set the machinery of his engagement in motion by taking a train to Berlin. Travel was in itself exhilarating, and as the miles clicked away he became more and more excited at the prospect of seeing Felice again and of doing something positive about his future. From the train station he took a subway to the local stop nearest her house. Getting out of the subway car he rushed across the platform and started up the steps leading to the street.

Felice had come down the steps to meet the train. As the young man with the intense dark eyes hurried past her, she recognized him and quickly put out her hand. And then there they stood, amid a swirl of commuters, Felice holding Franz quietly by the hand, smiling at him in greeting.

They became formally engaged. Franz felt the notice in the newspapers was rather unnerving. It seemed as if Felice were going to perform a bicycle stunt in the Variety Theatre; still he felt that their names looked natural and warm together. When the two returned to Prague, Franz got dressed in his best dark-blue suit and tight collar, and with Felice paid a formal call on Max Brod and his wife. (Max wrote later he was rather dismayed at the spectacle of Franz trying to conform as a perfectly proper fiancé.)

The next week, after a happy Felice had returned to Berlin, Franz confessed to Max that from the moment he had made the decision to get married he could no longer get any sleep. Being tied down to social conventions, paying family calls, dutiful conversations about the joys and sorrows of relatives—were beginning to smother him.

It must have occurred to Max Brod sometime in that year of 1912 that he wished Felice Bauer had never come from Berlin to Prague for her visit. And a similar emotion may have stirred in Kafka's own household; for, as he lay on the couch one late afternoon, his mother, that most mild-mannered and self-effacing of women, became volubly impatient with him.

She simply burst out in indignation, reproaching him for not appreciating her or his father's attempts to be good to him. Nobody understood him! She supposed she was a stranger to him; and both she and his father wished him nothing but harm!

Franz replied that of course he knew they didn't wish him any real harm, but that he did feel misunderstood. There's little doubt that Franz, nearly thirty and still living with his parents (in spite of all his love-hate-guilt feelings toward them) and unable to make up his mind about the great step of marriage, saw himself in a less-than-noble light. Nevertheless the strain of his indecision was beginning to show up physically. The brief spell of illness he had suffered two years before had been all but forgotten; but now some of the same symptoms were coming back: a tightness of the chest muscles, a slight difficulty in breathing. Franz ignored them, with a note in his diary to the effect that he was relieved that he had no desire to smoke cigarettes.

Eight

"DEAREST FATHER—"

Franz was to write this salutation more than once in his efforts to communicate with Herrmann Kafka, the man to whom he could scarcely say "good morning" without stammering. A letter written four years later was to be over a hundred pages in length, and to give in anguished and excruciating detail every facet of an answer to a question his father was to ask him: "Why are you afraid of me?" This first letter, however, had an entirely different tone—positive, almost joyful. In it Franz set forth a proposition for his father's approval. He had saved several hundred dollars out of his salary; also, thanks to Max Brod, he had sold several stories and articles; and now he thought that he would like to quit the company and go to Berlin to be close to his fiancée and see if, for the next couple of years at least, he could live on his savings and what money he might earn from future stories.

It was certainly a step in the right direction—toward life, toward realizing his potentialities both as a man capable of marriage and as a writer. The only trouble was that war was threatening Europe. The assassination of Archduke Francis Ferdinand of Austria-Hungary by a Serbian nationalist had set off a powder keg. Serbia as well as Russia was fanning Czech hopes for freedom; Germany was beginning to threaten France and Great Britain to even old scores over colonial territories. In August 1914 the Prague newspapers ran bold headlines: WAR DECLARED!

Thus it was the worst possible time for Franz Kafka to propose that he should quit his job and go to Germany to be with his fiancée and live on his savings. Most writers who have written about Franz Kafka have suspected that, at least subconsciously, Franz picked this time to declare his bid for freedom from bureaucracy, along with taking on the responsibility for the life of another person, when both were practically a foregone impossibility.

The war swept through Bohemia; Germany, Austria-Hungary, and Italy were joined in battle against France, Russia, England, and Japan. Because of his civil service job with the Workers' Accident Insurance Institution of Bohemia, Franz Kafka was not drafted (to his great relief, since he was a pacifist). But there was no possibility of quitting his job and traveling to Germany. Instead he remained in Prague, working harder than before. He re-acted to the war with predictable, empathetic worry; he would meet Max Brod after work with a newspaper clutched in his hand, and thunder about the latest "vil-lain," Italy, actually on the side of Germany, whose battle-ships were preparing to bombard a coast unprotected by heavy artillery and where they would therefore suffer great civilian casualties.

In 1915 in Prague, Czech barbers, who traditionally advertised their trade by hanging glittering brass shaving bowls, in the manner of Don Quixote (the mad knight who used a shaving bowl as a helmet, considering it di-vine), now painted their barbershop signs red, blue, and white, the colors of Bohemia, in an outburst of na-tional fervor to become an independent country. The Czechs of Prague also erected a statue in their Old Town Square to mark the 500th anniversary of the death of martyred John Huss, burned at the stake on that spot for having insisted that a Pope whom he knew to be immoral had no right to claim that his every pronouncement was infallible in the sight of God. John Huss now became a rallying point for the young Czechs who were holding meetings and marching to demand the independence of a new country to be called Czechoslovakia. Franz marched with them with enthusiasm, shying away only when they veered toward violence.

He began to spend his free hours in new discoveries, such as that of the Montessori system of childhood edu-cation, which he would certainly have wanted for any child of his. And he began to study the long, complex history of the Jews. By then he had realized that his

father, while still pretending to be a devout and knowl-
edgeable Jew, almost never went to the temple and had
hardly any interest in his own heritage. (One of Franz's
first scraps of information about Orthodox Jews was that
they were forbidden by ancient custom to read their Holy
Book, the Torah, on the Christian holy day of Christmas,
an observation, Franz felt, that gave too much importance
to this day; and he was very amused to read about the
rabbi who made a practice of saving that evening of
Christmas as the time to express his contempt by cutting
large quantities of newspapers into small squares—his
next year's supply of toilet paper!)

Franz, with Max and other young men, frequented the
local plays, appreciating such comedies as *The Good
Soldier Schweik* (pronounced *Schwake* in Czech) about
an orderly in the army who got away with outrageous behavior by pretending to be as stupid in the face of Authority as *he* felt Authority was. Franz loved the antics of
Schweik, and also those of the movie clown on the silent
screen, Charlie Chaplin. He saw Chaplin as the spokes-
man against the machine world, in which most men could
no longer manage to do what they liked with their lives.

Also in this period Franz occasionally took a young
woman named Gertrude, or "Trude," Thieberger to plays
and movies.

Years later, Trude (then Gertrude Urzidil) recalled
her meeting with Franz Kafka in 1915:

"It was three years after his first book, *Contemplation,*
was published. He brought me the book as we went to
the Prague Theatre to see a performance of the opera
Carmen. My parents would not have permitted me to go

with another young man, but they had no objections to my going with the exceptional Kafka. He did not bring the usual candies; instead he presented me with his *Contemplation,* in which he had inscribed a significant dedication."

The dedication contained a reference to the famous librettist, Prosper Merimée, who had written the words to the opera:

"For Trude Thieberger with my greetings and a suggestion. No flies will get into a closed mouth (last sentence of *Carmen* by Merimée). It has not been followed in the book. Therefore it is full of flies. The best would be to keep it closed."

"Such was Kafka's statement," Trude Thieberger was to write, "about a work which meant a new phase in European prose." But back in 1915 her main impression of Franz was that he certainly did love *Carmen,* with its passionate story of the cigarette factory girl and the bullfighter, of love and violent death, set against the hot harsh colors of Spain. It is not unusual for someone enthusiastic over a particular opera to see it more than once, but Franz was so enraptured with *Carmen* that he took Trude to see it practically every time it was performed.

But soon Franz stopped calling on Trude. He was disturbed at the letters coming from Berlin; Felice had written that her family was wondering when they would set the date for their marriage.

Franz met his friend Max Brod at their favorite café, the Arco, with its photographs and paintings of famous people. And Franz tried to sum up all his reasons for getting married. How bitter life would be if he remained a bachelor. To have to invite someone to one's house for the sake of nothing but spending an evening, and then to have to say good-night at the door. And when one was ill, to be quite alone. And never to have the joy of running up the stairs beside one's pretty wife. And to have to live in other people's houses, having to pass apologetically through their living rooms, carrying one's supper home in a bag from some shop. And admiring other people's children without even being able to earn a little sympathy by saying "we" have none of our own.

It did not seem to occur to Franz that most of his reasons in favor of marriage were negative ones; and Max Brod thought it would be useless to point this out. Instead, he tried to think of a good example of a positive sort. He didn't dare use his own marriage, which, although it was happy, was plagued at the time with money troubles. But then Max discovered another example right in front of him. Franz was sitting in his favorite place, under the large portrait of Thomas Alva Edison. The signed picture was inscribed: "The Wizard of Menlo Park." Edison had visited Prague in 1911, and besides introducing the arc light for street lighting, had given the city its first electric streetcars. Kafka was a great admirer of Edison; and now Max reminded him that there was a man of enormous creative ability who had time to invent many things despite the fact that he had been married twice and had four or five children. Franz seemed rather impressed by this example, since Edison was one of his few scientific heroes. (As Trude Thieberger's future husband, Johannes Urzidil, was to write: "Edison and [Benjamin] Franklin represented to Kafka the Great American Dream Wish.")

That same year Franz was surprised and gratified to be

presented with a small literary award for his story, "The Stoker." The prize had originally been presented to another, more established author, but he had relinquished it in order that it might be given to a bright new name, "F. Kafka." Franz was encouraged by this generous gesture from a fellow writer, and he plunged into one of his most ambitious undertakings, a book to be known as *The Trial*.

As was his habit, when he had finished the first chapter, he needed the criticism—good as well as bad—of his friends before going further. As Max Brod noted, when Kafka read aloud (and reading one's story, rather than giving the hastily written and perhaps unreadable script to others, was the custom in those times before typewriters were common) his humor became especially clear. Max reports that in the first chapter of *The Trial,* despite its fearful earnestness, the humor was so bitingly apparent that Franz's listeners laughed heartily. Later Max marveled at that laughter, because he knew that the first chapter of *The Trial* was in deadly earnest. It concerned a young man named Joseph K. One morning while about to be served his breakfast by the landlady, he is confronted by two men in tight, official-looking black uniforms who say he is under arrest. He will be allowed to continue in his job as head clerk in a large bank but he will have to stay in town to be at the constant disposal of the court. Although Joseph K. doesn't at first feel any guilt, the pending trial slowly awakens this feeling in him. He seeks relief from his anxieties with a Fräulein Bürstner, who, while not objecting to his advances, is unable to help him solve his dilemma.

The idea of a simple, law-abiding, and peace-loving man who goes quietly about his own business, being arrested abruptly by officials who don't even tell him what his crime has been, yet kept in an indefinite state of suspense and suspicion until he believes he must indeed be guilty of some criminal act—was the situation that struck Max Brod and even Franz Kafka himself as humorous—what today might well be called "black" humor. It was ludicrous, wasn't it? And yet there was that element lurking behind it of "It *could* happen, anytime." But what neither Franz nor his listening friends could have known was that *The Trial* opened the door, in the year the First World War was declared, to a look into the far grimmer realities of the Second. Years later, Max Brod watched while the Nazis took over much of Europe and Storm Troopers began pounding on the doors of innocent citizens during the night to take men from their families and put them to death without a trial. It seemed to Max that Kafka must have witnessed such a possibility in a dream, that moment of arrest—or how else could he have captured with terrible perfection the atmosphere of dread and hopelessness, and even dressed his arrestors in the tight-fitting buckled and belted leathery black uniforms that he described?

Of course the "transference" of Kafka into "Joseph K.," the "K." standing for Kafka; and again the "F.B." of "Fräulein Bürstner" for Felice Bauer, were, by now, recognizable Kafka clues. But in *The Trial* the symbolism of the story mirroring the actual life is clear to any reader aware of the basic facts about Kafka. Joseph K. at last receives a summons to court, and has the chance to meet with someone, a lawyer, who can probably help him. But he misses his opportunity because he leaves the room to make love to the lawyer's nurse. Joseph K. is never brought to trial but is now convinced of his own guilt. Two messengers of the court come to see him, with their courteous manners which only increase the horror; and just before they ceremoniously stab him to death, an act which he doesn't in the least protest, he catches sight of the figure of—he's almost sure it is—Fräulein Bürstner.

Most critics assume that Franz was condemning himself for a crime that society hadn't mentioned but which was taken for granted, the crime of being unable to go ahead and marry one's betrothed. And furthermore, in the story he goes out with another young woman, one who does not demand that the liaison has to end in a legally binding tie. This double crime of course will have to be paid for; and as always with its author, paid for by the grimmest of penalties, death.

Sometimes in his stories Kafka wrote of events after they had happened; but mostly, as in the case of *The Trial,* before. The same year he became engaged to Felice Bauer he broke the engagement off; and shortly thereafter had an affair with another woman who had never mentioned marriage.

Ironically, she was a friend of Felice Bauer's, sent by Felice from Berlin to see what could be done to repair the damage to the marriage plans. Her name was Grete Bloch. In many ways she reminded Franz of the absent Felice; she also was a businesswoman, proud and independent, but with a great difference; she listened to Franz's agonized pros and cons about marriage without any evident emotional involvement of her own. It was a relief for Franz as he poured out his impassioned feelings about two people living in close proximity, with their individual feelings of being basically strangers, pitying each other's weaknesses and recognizing their own cowardice and vanity, and only in their deepest subconscious perhaps aware of a trickling stream that could honestly be called love. Franz confessed that he felt the relationship between himself and Felice would mean that the two of them would have to "blast a road through the rocks" of their differences. Perhaps, he thought, it was not the idea of marriage that kept him so hesitant; perhaps it was Felice herself, with her special needs and demands. For instance, she had insisted on his providing a comfortable house for her, an interest in his father's business, good meals every day, and central heating. Not only that, but she had reset his watch, which he was in the habit of keeping an hour and a half fast—admittedly in his nervous desire never to be late for work. (There is no evidence of whether Fräulein Bloch supported Felice Bauer in her own disapproval of anybody who insisted on setting his watch so far ahead of time.) Franz added that Felice had corrected the bad German he had used to a Berlin waiter; she had called his sisters, Valli and Elli, shallow; she hadn't even asked after the youngest, Ottla, who had become his favorite; and above all she never asked any questions about his writing and evidently had no interest in it.

And so it was that in the year 1914 Grete Bloch, in the role of mediator between her friend Felice and Franz Kafka, had a short affair with Franz and then went back to Germany. After several letters back and forth, Grete abruptly broke off all correspondence, and Franz never heard from her again. He did not try to continue contact, perhaps from a sense of unease at having become involved with Felice's close friend. But there is a postscript to the story of Grete Bloch in the life of Franz Kafka, that was not to be written until after Franz's death.

This short, no doubt guilt-ridden, relationship with Grete had its immediate effect on Franz. He was inspired to write "In the Penal Colony." It is a story of breathtaking originality, powerful imagery, and vicarious torment in which every reader is forced to participate. Surely World War I, as well as Kafka's own war with himself, was a factor.

In an unnamed country, at an unspecified time, an old commandant invents a machine for the death punishment. The condemned is placed face down in this machine and the reason for his sentence is written, driven, with needles across and into his back. Slowly during his agony he comes to "read" the script written with a flourish across his bleeding flesh, until hours later, approaching death, he understands the meaning of the message and then dies, presumably in peace. At the end of the story the official who operates the machine finds that it has gone haywire and is not killing in the proper fashion. As a matter of correct procedure, he substitutes himself for the victim and lets the wildly erratic instrument write on his naked back its by now senseless message, until it has penetrated his vital organs and has thrown him into the pit below.

What Kafka seems to be saying is: If you put yourself

in charge of terrible things it is only fitting that you be destroyed by them.

In that same year of 1914 Kafka finally left his parents' house. The step was a small one; he moved to the apartment of another family in which he rented a room. Usually he took his evening meal with the family, just as he had done with his own. Perhaps there was one small advantage: the family carried on its own arguments at the table, but at least they had nothing to do with Franz.

He was still fighting the battle of To Get Married or Not. He told Max Brod that he could imagine exactly what it would be like. He and Felice would have the usual two-room apartment; in one of them his working wife would rise early and run off to work, to fall dead-tired on her bed in the evening; in the other room there would be a sofa, where the laggard F. Kafka would loll around, out of work, writing and dreaming, and feeding himself on milk and honey. Franz felt that the familiar European saying fitted the situation: "There he lies and takes his ease, the man whom morals do not tease."

By July 1916, Franz was again courting Felice Bauer. He had a short vacation and had persuaded her to meet him at the romantic spa of Marienbad. Franz, still nervous about committing himself in the matter of marriage, talked mostly of his worry about the war. It was burning and tearing up the world. He actually wept with rage over the plight of the poor, such as an account he had read in the newspaper of the trial of a twenty-three-year-old woman named Marie Abraham who, facing starvation and being evicted from her miserable room, strangled her nine-month-old child. Franz was frustrated that he could do nothing about victims such as this poor mother, or for soldiers who were dying at the front.

When he returned to Prague he went to his superiors at the Workers' Accident Insurance Institution and began a long and persistent campaign to have them sponsor a sanitorium, or rest home, for soldiers who were coming home from battle shell-shocked, unable to resume their civilian lives. After months of Kafka's gentle, courteous, but stubborn perseverance, the officials gave him his way and the sanitorium was established.

Franz was immensely heartened by the opening of the sanitorium; it was undeniable proof that he could propose a project and carry it through. In his current state of mind he felt that perhaps he could, after all, take on the responsibilities of marriage. And so, in 1917, Franz again became engaged to Felice Bauer, this time in spite of her family's objections.

The marriage date was set. Franz sat at his desk in the insurance office and thought about the changes that would soon begin in his life. He would be coming home every day, no longer to his own quiet room where his writing materials waited, but to a room where there would always be somebody else, who would want to be talked to and taken places. And soon there would probably be a child, and after that, another and another, crowding the apartment. Franz kept telling himself that he would like that, even if they interfered with his writing. He had always loved the *idea* of being a father.

At work Franz was discovering that almost every time he tried to carry on a conversation it would end in a

Kafka with Felice Bauer, photographed when they became engaged for the second time in the summer of 1917.

coughing attack. Sometimes the attack lasted for several minutes, while the man sharing his office, Herr Treml, glared over at him, and Franz, stammering apologies, only coughed the harder. Before the year was out he was to hear a grave warning from a doctor, and a dreadful word.

Tuberculosis.

Nine

FRANZ WAS STARTLED out of sleep at about four in the morning by a violent fit of coughing. To his surprise he found he was coughing up blood. He walked to his window and back to his washstand trying to overcome the attack.

At seven o'clock, after perhaps only twenty minutes of sleep, he got up and went off to work as usual. Later that same day he mentioned rather offhandedly to Max Brod that he had been coughing up blood, that he had been somewhat stimulated as one would be by anything new, and of course a little alarmed.

Brod was horrified. Coughing blood! He should have gone straight to a doctor! Franz replied that he couldn't stand doctors, with their prescribing of "unnatural" medicines.

Max kept after Franz, whose attacks continued almost every night. After two weeks, Franz, whom Max was calling "unbelievably pigheaded," gave in primarily because he was too exhausted to go to work, and let Max take him to a doctor. Professor Friedl Pick examined the thin young man with the racking cough, and diagnosed severe inflammation of the lungs, with danger of tuberculosis. He suggested that Franz leave the city immediately, where the air pollution from heavy industry was bad for him, and rest for at least three months.

Franz hesitated about asking his employers for such a long leave of absence, especially if he were obliged to tell them the cause. Surely then they would dismiss him! He remembered only too well his father's reaction to the employee who was frequently absent because of TB, and how Herrmann Kafka had declared that the sooner the fellow died the better. But Max kept after Franz and finally he got up the courage to ask for the leave. It was promptly granted.

Max took his friend to a small resort outside the city, where there was a swimming pool. There Franz found he was too weak from coughing to challenge Max to races across the pool, as he had so often in the past, but lying in the sun made him feel very good. Max had to go on working but he went to the resort on weekends, and the two of them would stretch out by the pool and talk. Franz didn't want to discuss his illness except for his attitude toward it, which was an odd combination of wonder and affection. He had come to an interesting conclusion: that his lungs had been responding in sympathy to his brain, which had been wrestling with the problem of whether or not to get married. The brain had no longer been able to endure the strain of worry, of decisions, and had said, in effect, "I give up!" And the lungs, in alarm, had been trying to warn him. Franz marveled at this silent and terrible dialogue that had taken place, unknown to himself, until it erupted in noise and blood.

Max agreed that Franz's long struggle over whether or not to marry had probably weakened his body's defenses, thus allowing the disease to take hold. But Franz was still musing over the "wonder" of what had happened to him. Didn't Max understand, his body had actually provided him with a solution to his dilemma, by making him so ill that he couldn't get married if he wanted to, at least until he recovered. Franz could even joke about it, saying that God must have heard him crying out for a solution, and sent him one, although it *was* a bit drastic, and (here he quoted from a Wagnerian opera) he would have taken Him for more of a gentleman. In the same slightly hysterical vein that this illness had brought upon Franz, he added that he had decided that after he was well again he would certainly attempt to be married. In fact, if he was still single at the age of forty he would marry just anybody, even an old man with buckteeth!

Max couldn't help pointing out, as a good friend, Franz's behavior in the past year. Having got himself engaged for the second time to the same woman, what had he done? When he should have been looking for an apartment for himself and Felice, he had, instead, moved away from the family whose apartment he'd been sharing, and into a single room. Then he'd found that this room was on a noisy courtyard, and had moved again, taking an even smaller, quieter room in the Street of Alchemists (in a quaint medieval quarter). And then Franz had moved a third time into a small place that had a private garden so that he need not even venture out in the evening and be jostled by people on the streets. It seemed utterly clear to Max that these were not the actions of a man who could ever bring himself to marry; but who, on the contrary, was fleeing toward more and more privacy and quiet.

Franz Kafka's mood became a little less lighthearted. With his writer's imagination his friend's words conjured up a picture—a frightening picture of a man running in a maze of rooms which got smaller and narrower, until he reached the final place, which was so small that there was only room for him to lie down—his coffin. Franz turned quickly away from that image, but later that day he began on another story. It was a story he did not want to end the way it did, but it took on a life of its own, and in spite of Franz's belief that he would indeed get married as soon as he was well, the story had it otherwise.

A prince comes with his bride before his father, the king, and says that he cannot go on with his princely duties. He is overcome by nausea when he goes out on the balcony to make speeches, he can't breathe the air outside, and it's too noisy there. The king reminds him that he had taken on these obligations before his wedding. The princess takes her husband's side, and agrees that the prince's life is now a burden; that he must always be ready to carry out his responsibilities, which means that at a moment's notice he must struggle into his tight regulation uniform, which is repulsively bright, almost theatrical, almost dishonorable. When he returns to the princess he sometimes can barely get in the door before he collapses. Now the prince puts it to his father whether it is possible for anyone to go on living like that.

"Woman's talk," the king snaps. And at that point of dreadful indecision, the author abandons his story.

When Franz's three months' leave was over, he was feeling much better. He returned to the office; he also returned to his father's house. He wanted to explain his position to his parents, wanted them to understand (and approve of) the reasons for his prolonged indecision. Franz saw his father as an example of a man who, despite his tyrannical ways, possessed the virtues of industry, endurance, presence of mind, and fearlessness. And if such a man had had to fight hard, and as far as raising his children was concerned, had been a failure, how could he, his son, who possessed none of these virtues, hope to make a success of marriage?

Of course Franz, in his miserable stammer, could not speak out and tell his father that he had set a pretty bad example. But, at the dining room table, the scene of so many of Herrmann's tirades, he asked for his parents' advice.

His father said curtly that Franz should marry. Every man should be married, it was what society expected of him.

His mother, as usual, echoed her husband. But then she reinforced his opinion that Franz ought to be married.

"Marriage," remarked Julie Kafka, "would reduce that

writing of yours to the dose that cultivated people need."

No comment could have shown more clearly the lack of appreciation, even of patience, with which Franz's parents regarded his true life's work.

Franz's reaction was a strange one. Instead of going ahead with the marriage, he broke within days his second and final engagement to Felice Bauer. And to help explain himself to Felice and her parents, he begged his own parents to come with him to Berlin. It seemed almost as if Franz were saying, "Your advice about marriage convinced me I couldn't go through with it. Now you must help me get out of it!"

Somewhat to Franz's surprise, Herrmann and Julie Kafka came along. Perhaps they wanted to show the well-to-do and respected parents of their son's long-suffering fiancée that they, at least, were just as respectable and knew their duty, such as apologizing for the behavior of their son.

On that unusual visit Franz's normally loud and quick-tempered father was the soul of dignity and quiet understanding. He explained to Felice's father that Franz was in very poor health, worse off than his appearance might lead one to believe, and so it was probably a blessing that this fact was faced before anything so permanent as a marriage could take place.

Franz's response to this was a joyful burst of admiration and gratitude. He wrote (in that famous long letter to his father which was supposed to be one long cry of reproach) of how, on the train to Berlin, his father had to sit up all night in his shirt-sleeves—not a word, however, of his mother's equal sacrifice of comfort. And then he wrote of how his father had spoken so splendidly on his behalf and conveyed his, Franz's, regrets about the situation so much better than he could ever have done.

With the ordeal of confronting Felice's parents and the five-year relationship with Felice finally behind him, Franz came back to Prague—and stumbled into the office of his best friend. He fell into a chair beside Max's desk and in spite of there being three or four other people in the room, broke down in a fit of weeping. He said that he had displayed meanness, indecision, caution, and counting the cost—the soul of a petty clerk, that was all he was, at the Workers' Accident Insurance Institution—such a pitifully meager soul! And then there came a really terrible attack of coughing.

Ten

"YOU WILL HAVE TO ENTER a TB sanitorium," advised the doctor. There was no doubt anymore about Franz having contracted tuberculosis.

Franz was again pigheaded. But his favorite sister, Ottla, came to the rescue. She had taken over the management of a small rest home at Zürau, outside Prague (over the objections of their father who wanted his daughters to remain financially dependent on him). Ottla persuaded her brother to come out to the bracing country air at Zürau, vowing she would nurse him back to health.

Franz went, and sunned himself on a small terrace with a few other people, speaking to none of them. He was still thinking of Felice Bauer.

Felice had passed out of his life, but not entirely out of his thoughts. Two years later she was to write to Max Brod that she had married. As for all the correspondence that flew back and forth between Prague and Berlin, Felice's letters were destroyed, perhaps because of her former lover's sense of inadequacy. Franz's own letters, with their alternating moods of love, hope, reluctance, and despair, can be read, although at present they have not been translated and published in English.

Franz was still at Zürau in 1918 when World War I ended. Soon after that the monarchy that had been Austria-Hungary was broken up and Bohemia became a province of the new Czechoslovakia. Max Brod wrote Franz about the parades and dancing in the streets of Prague, of the flower garlands hung around the statue of the martyred John Huss. From Zürau, Franz replied that he was thankful for the Czechs who had finally won a home of their own; but he did not feel that the new country would make any difference in his life. For Franz still thought of himself as less a Czech than a Jew.

Franz also received a letter from an official at the insurance company saying that he had "almost" been awarded a decoration by the government for his efforts in setting up the sanitorium for shell-shocked servicemen. The inference was that since he had not been in the army he was not "quite" eligible.

His sister did not succeed in curing him but he was improving somewhat in the clear country air. And he had embarked on a most ambitious book, the inspiration for which had come to him one evening when he had been invited to the house of a landowner known around the countryside as Farmer Lüftner. Franz described the suppertime scene in a letter to Max so well that Max felt he had been there himself. A great long room, and the landowner, a character right out of feudal times, banging his beer tankard on the table, roaring with laughter, talking with passion about shooting game; and in the stable his two gigantic horses, like figures out of a heroic saga, glimpsed in a fleeting ray of sun that streamed through the window. One can imagine the frail, tubercular young man caught up in this atmosphere of lusty good health, rough laughter, and enjoyment of the physical life. He could no longer become a part of it but he could absorb its energies, its powerful impressions, and make them into a book.

It was to be called *The Castle*. Here Kafka, portraying the character he knows best—himself—calls the young man simply "K." K. goes to a strange village where he hopes to take on a job as a land surveyor and find new friends. But nobody knows of such a job or wants to be his friend. However, the town's women are attracted to him, and this makes the men show even greater resentment and hostility. To live in this town K. has to get the permission of officials in the Castle, but although he can see it he cannot seem to reach the place. All roads lead to the Castle; and yet, as he walks along them, they turn aside, to his frustration, and never lead him any closer than when he started out. K. admits to a schoolmaster that he doesn't feel he belongs in the company of the peasants, townspeople, or the rulers in the Castle. The schoolmaster says that there is really no difference between the peasants and the people of the Castle, thus convincing K. that he really doesn't belong anywhere.

The theme of *The Castle* might be called "the eternal quest," in this case, the quest to reach the Castle. In a larger sense this quest is man's seeking after the ultimate answer—proof of God, a sort of final Truth. There's a dreamlike quality about *The Castle,* and Kafka's quest reminds many a reader of a familiar dream in which one is traveling down a seemingly endless road, searching for "the answer to the universe." Psychiatrists often encounter this need on the part of a patient for "the answer" that will, in one word, provide the solution to the mysteries of everything in life.

Some readers have seen the Castle as Kafka's true home which he could never find; and in a larger sense, the rightful home of the Jews. While the word "Jew" is never mentioned in *The Castle,* the story of the lonely outsider in an unfriendly town where the people are not like himself is deeply Jewish in its special sense of rootlessness, with the promised land tantalizingly in sight yet always out of reach.

Parallel to *The Castle* Franz wrote a shorter story he called "Homecoming," which was much plainer and more poignant in its imagery. He saw himself as having returned to his father's house; he sees the smoke rising from the chimney, smells coffee being made for supper. And he wonders who will come out to greet him from this house of his childhood. He doesn't dare knock at the door for fear of discovering there will be no welcome. The longer he hesitates before the door, the more of a stranger he feels, until finally he is fearful that, while he lingers there in indecision, someone *will* open the door and then he will know he is useless to them. The warmth of their fireplace and the hospitality of their coffee will not be for him.

In his continuing longing to go back, to return to the place of his childhood and establish himself as an important part of that setting—even though he had found that it was to no avail—Franz conjures up other writers, before and after himself—from Marcel Proust, with his *Remembrance of Things Past,* to Thomas Wolfe's *You Can't Go Home Again.* The urge to "go home again," especially if one has never, in one's opinion, properly belonged in the family, is one of the most compelling and haunting longings that anyone can have.

The next year, thanks to his sister Ottla's care, Franz was much improved and he returned to Prague, where his story, "In the Penal Colony," was published.

And in that same year, 1919, Franz met another woman—and again contemplated marriage! He had convinced himself that it was Felice Bauer's middle-class concepts, with all the proprieties and conventions strictly observed, that had made him unable to put the rest of his life into her hands. Now here was someone altogether different. There is almost nothing of Julie Wohryzek in Franz's diaries, but she seems to have been a much less conventional and demanding young woman than her predecessor. Again, Franz became engaged.

This time his father, who had said that Franz should be married, was thoroughly exasperated with him. He made a big scene in which he said that Franz was a grown man with presumably a mind of his own, a city man, and what does he do? He is attracted to the next pretty girl he sees, who has dressed herself up in a fancy blouse—something those Prague Jewesses were good at—and right away his son wants to marry her! The best explanation that one can give for Herrmann Kafka's outburst is that he saw himself in the position, sooner or later, of having to go again to the parents of a jilted girl and apologize for his son's breaking the engagement.

Old Herrmann was at least half right; he was not called upon to intercede with Julie Wohryzek's parents, but the engagement was broken within two months. During that time Julie had found a place for the presumably young married couple to live. And there was Franz, sitting on the sofa of this small, one-room apartment, which was to be theirs in a week and considering with a claustrophobic dread the prospect of living in such cramped quarters with another person, and also considering with rising panic how it was *he* who had urged this marriage, over Julie's nervous resistance. In despair he began to try to explain about his fears, how he had been hoping that someday he might be able to quit working and devote his time to writing, but married, especially with children— how could this ever be? Franz looked at his young fiancée as if he thought it possible that she might have an answer. But Julie had no answers.

Alone again, Franz felt the usual wave of relief sweep over him, having succeeded once more in keeping his life fairly uncomplicated. He said to Max that he was about ready to admit that life as a bachelor, empty though it might be, probably suited him best; for already he was able to talk to himself again! And, besides, he knew that living such a life would be the only way that he might finally recover from the sickness still lodged in his lungs.

He plunged again into the only real release he was

ever to experience—writing his stories of people balanced on the edge of madness, such as a trapeze artist who stays forever on his high perch in the circus tent, not needing to come down into the world below, but trembling with fear because he has only one bar to hang onto; and how could he bear to go on with his dangerous performances? Then there was the story, "Eleven Sons," with its different personalities who were kind, clever, fragile, elegant, insecure—various elements of himself, and further revelation of his wish to have children of his own. Kafka turned animals into humans, humans into animals, with biting satirical results, usually at the expense of the humans. He understood the humiliations of poverty, as in his story "The Bucket Rider," in which a man makes a fool of himself by "riding" his bucket to the coal dealer to beg for a shovelful of the cheapest coal, and is mocked by the dealer's wife.

In one of his most profound stories, "The Next Village," he sums up a philosophy of life in just one paragraph. He has the character of his own grandfather saying how astoundingly short life is; it seems so short, in fact, that he, the old man, cannot understand how a young man can decide to ride over to the next village without being afraid that—aside from accidents—even the span of a normal happy life might fall far short of the time needed for such a journey.

Franz Kafka's own time was running out. Yet ahead of him still lay meetings with three people who were to become important to him, and whose lives he was to change forever.

The first of these was Milena.

Eleven

In 1920, Prague, for all its ancient history and beauty, was still a provincial town; but in the German section it had a stylish promenade called the Corso. On Sunday mornings smartly dressed Germans, students, Austrian officers, strolled up and down, smiling, greeting one another, conducting business. Usually towering above the throng was the governor of Prague, the six-foot-six Count Thun, who stood on one of his stork-thin legs, one knee tucked into the back of the other, surveying the scene through a black-rimmed monocle. On one such sunny morning two girls came along, and there was a stir of excitement and curiosity in the crowd. One newspaper reporter of the time was inspired to write about them; he considered them a sensational sight, the first Prague girls who had set out to look boyish. They were probably the forerunners of the new postwar generation, who were extending the boundaries of their world from the Czech section of the city to the Corso, and so had made contact with the young German literary generation. They were introduced as Milena Jesenká and her sister.

One of those members of the literary generation, now not so young at age thirty-nine, was Franz Kafka. Milena was only twenty-four but already a respected journalist who wrote for a Prague newspaper. She had read Kafka's published stories, and now she proposed translating them from German into her native Czech.

In discussions over these translations the two would meet at favorite places around the city, such as the beautiful old cobbled streets that led down to the river. They boarded a trolley, on which there was often a merry, bony old conductor. Franz observed how the children aboard oohed and ahed at him in admiration of the way he performed his duties; and Franz declared that he would like nothing better than to be such a conductor, powerful and respected, driving around the city with his foot on the outside board, bending over the children to punch their tickets, gay and a part of everything. With Milena he found himself laughing again as he hadn't since the days on vacation with Max. He teased his new girl friend; was it true what he'd heard about her, that she spent her money like a gypsy; and she had swum the Moldau at night on a dare? Milena admitted to all.

She was married, with a home in Vienna, but she was unhappy, as her husband was having affairs with other women. She had no money except what she made as a journalist, and she also worked as a porter in the Vienna railroad station, carrying other people's baggage. Her father, a Gentile, was a millionaire but he would not give her a penny because she had married a Jew.

It is possible that Milena's being married allowed Franz, with all his indecisions about marriage, to let himself fall in love in a way that he never had before. Another reason that he was drawn to Milena was that she felt toward other people the same almost painful sensitivity that he did. He had told her the story of how he had run around and around the Old Town Square in an attempt to give the old beggar woman his small coins, so that she might think that several boys were arriving with one coin apiece. Milena then told him about her first kiss. At age fourteen she'd visited an old friend of the family who was in the hospital after an eye operation. She brought him, dutifully, a bunch of violets; then she saw that his eyes were bandaged; and realizing that he couldn't see the flowers she wanted to give him something right away that he could appreciate, so she'd kissed him, but the kiss landed on his nose, and ended up on his chin. Tears streamed down Milena's face and onto the old man's as she stammered she hadn't meant it like that. But when she got home she found the telegraph office had delivered a large bouquet of flowers with a note that told her that the patient had understood her good intentions perfectly.

Franz admired Milena for her intelligence, tenderness, and bravery of spirit, and he wrote of her as "a living fire." After a few idyllic days in Prague, she was obliged by her journalistic responsibilities to return to Vienna. From there she began to write letters entreating Franz to come and visit her. He longed to but he kept putting this off, wary, no doubt, about becoming "the other man" in a divorce suit with the subsequent commitment to marriage.

But the letters between Kafka and Milena became material for Franz's diary, and thus enriched the body of work he left for those who would appreciate him later. Franz wrote delightfully of the sensation of having a telegram from Milena in his pocket. It was always new—for the moment he had absorbed its contents the paper became blank—but he had only to stick it back in his pocket for the words to be written on it again.

Milena's letters kept encouraging Franz to come to Vienna, promising him that they could find a place in seclusion for his visit. Franz pleaded that he couldn't get away from the insurance company so soon after the absences caused by his illness. Milena suggested a telegram that would read that a hypothetical Aunt Clara was ill and that he should come at once. Franz's reply: Did she think he could go to the head official and, with a straight face, tell him about Aunt Clara? Of course, all Jews had their Aunt Claras, but his had died some time ago. He added that Milena must realize this office of his was not just any old stupid institution (though it was, he quickly admitted, but perhaps more fantastic than stupid). But it had been his life up to then, and he couldn't treat it shabbily.

Was this an honest effort on Franz's part to be loyal to the office, which he loathed, or did he use it as an excuse to keep from coming to a decision with Milena? He thought of yet another reason for not going to Vienna— the long distance from Prague, the great effort of traveling all night on a train.

Milena made another effort; she wrote of her loneliness, especially in the intellectual sense, for the company of her "Frank," as she called him. Franz replied that if one lonely person joined up with another one it never led to a "being-at-home, but to a *Katorga*," a Russian word meaning a long term of imprisonment followed by exile. "One loneliness reflects itself in the other, even in the deepest, darkest night."

And then he brought another weapon to bear, against the idea of marrying Melina. After all, she was a Protestant, married to a Jew of whom her family didn't approve. He, Kafka, was also a Jew. In fact, Kafka considered himself the most typical Western-type Jew of all. Jews, he wrote to this Gentile woman, considered themselves allowed to own only what they could hold in their hands or between their teeth. Only tangible possessions gave them the right to be alive, and they would never again repossess whatever they lost, but instead, it would calmly sail away from them forever. Part of Franz's new consciousness of himself as a Jew stemmed from the fact that Prague at that time was experiencing the terrible impact of the inflation that was sweeping postwar Europe. Money was almost worthless, and both the Czech and German Gentiles in Prague were blaming the situation on their perennial scapegoats, the Jews. Franz had moved to another lonely room. From its front window he watched mounted police, bayonets at the ready, on guard against a crowd screaming for revenge against the Jews, which Franz knew included himself. He wrote Milena of the disgrace he felt at having to live under police protection. He heard Jews being called filthy rabble, and wondered if it was not the natural thing to leave a city where one was so despised; staying in such a place reminded him in self-disgust of cockroaches that can't be exterminated from a room.

He was able to escape the riots going on in Prague by being ordered again by his doctor to leave the city for the sake of his health. While at a rest home he wrote Milena to beware of his company. His disease was still with him, in his left lung. But after a stay in the mountains Franz returned to Prague feeling almost cured. By then his longing to be with the lovely journalist who loved him was so great that, frail as he felt, he attempted the long journey to Vienna.

Franz and Milena had four days in Vienna together, in which they walked hand in hand in the beautiful city, ran through flowery meadows, followed paths in the woods, and were relaxed and happy. Franz wore a white shirt open at the neck; his tan made him look quite healthy, and he was hardly coughing at all. By the end of this blissful stay he was thinking of the TB as a small, short-lived discomfort.

Then he returned to Prague and his job. And the illness grew rapidly worse; again blood appeared when Franz coughed.

At the office the head official reassured him as to how valuable his services were. But Franz was beginning to suffer all day with splitting headaches. He told his friend Max that it was the sort of feeling a pane of glass must

Kafka (foreground, right) *at rest home.*

have when it cracked; and that it did not seem as if he would ever leave the insurance office except for "galloping" tuberculosis. But in his continuing correspondence with Milena he kept the tone tender and gay. Her letters brought him the scent of the forest where they had walked and dallied—he could hear the wind in her sleeves! He would like to kiss the little hand that labored at doing his translations, and was obliged to carry luggage at the train station—kiss that hand so long that never again would it have to work either at his translations or any menial labor.

Milena wrote of her desire to get a divorce and marry her Frank. Franz replied by recounting a recent dream. In it, Milena had somehow caught fire. He had grabbed up an old coat and tried to smother the flames. Suddenly it was he who was on fire, and the coat wasn't helping. Then the fire brigade arrived, and put out the flames. But Milena was different from before, like a ghost, and she fell lifeless—or was it fainting?—into his arms. Surely such a dream was saying, "Don't try to come closer to me, Milena, you'll get burned—and so will I."

Franz's tone grew progressively more frantic in his attempt to hold onto Milena and yet keep her mostly at the distance that lay between Prague and Vienna. He wrote her about another dream, very sensual, in which he was a forest animal. (This may have been inspired by the idyllic walks they had taken in the Vienna woods.) He, the wild animal, had basked in the sunlight of her love but felt unworthy of this and had to return to the darkness of the deep woods. He had begun to run as fast as he could but with the deep desire to take his love along with him, and yet with the terrible doubt that if he went back for her, he would never find the darkness that meant safety to him.

And alone in his Prague rooming house Franz wrote in his notebooks and diary. It seemed to him that he and Milena were in one room with opposite doors, and each of them held the handle of one door, tensely, as if the need to escape might become intolerable. If one of the two occupants made the slightest of moves, the other instantly dashed behind his door. The room, in Kafka's tormented imagination, was one which, door handle or not, the persons in it could never leave. This image of being in a constricted space with somebody else, with the knowledge that one can never escape, is, again, Kafka's fear of marriage. And this theme of there being "no exit" to a room has been used by other famous writers who came after Kafka.

After two years of "Dear Frank," and "Dear Milena," Franz felt close to emotional exhaustion, just as he had after the long period of engagement to Felice Bauer. He found it was a relief when a day passed without a letter to excite and irritate him and he could do a little writing and look forward to sleep. The sleep was always disturbed by his coughing, but at least he did not have to lie in bed going over Milena's latest loving reproaches. Was he willing to lose her entirely? was Milena's ultimate challenge.

Franz, who'd recently read *Robinson Crusoe,* replied as if he were the shipwrecked mariner; Robinson, he said, had to sign on, make the dangerous voyage, be marooned on the island, find his friend Friday and eventually be rescued; but without Milena he would still be cast adrift on the island. And yet he added that there was something terribly dangerous in building so much on one person, and so fear was present from the beginning.

Franz was not yet forty but his deep-black hair grew gray at the temples. He felt as if there were weights on his shoulders, weights that would drag him down into deep water, and anyone trying to rescue him would give up, not from inability but from annoyance at the drowning man's own stupidity in not helping himself.

His coughing did not let up but grew deeper, so that he came out of every spasm with a faint surprise that he was still able to draw air into his lungs. He was forced to face the fact that he would have to go back to some sort of rest home. Not a sanitorium, where they gave injections! One clerk in the office had gone to such a place with a slight cough and had died there. And there was Franz's dislike of eating meat. He wrote to Milena of his apprehension of being in the hands of a doctor who would force him to swallow large quantities of meat in the name of his getting well. Even the idea of traveling from Prague to a sanitorium a couple of hundred miles away was appalling to Franz. Who would tolerate him in the sleeping car of a train when he coughed from the early, exhausted hour of 9:45 P.M. until 11:00; then at 12:00, when turning from the right side to the left, began to cough again and went on until 1:00 A.M.? There followed, to Milena, a complaint about the difference in prices between one sanitorium and another. All, Franz felt, were outrageous, and he was afraid both of losing his job and of costing his family money. Finally he talked himself into never leaving Prague to be at the mercy of strangers.

When the end was near, he wrote, he would have himself carried to Max Brod's house to discuss a vacation holiday lasting several days, because he felt so strong. And then he would crawl home to stretch himself out for the last time, and finally a man with a telegram about his death would climb Milena's long staircase.

Despite his worsening health, Franz remained at the insurance company and kept answering Milena's letters, although he had given up hope of gathering enough strength, physical and mental, to go again to Vienna.

At a later date Milena confided some of her fears about Franz to Max Brod.

It seemed to Milena that for her "Frank," life was just not the same kind of day-by-day experience that it was for ordinary people. For instance, he had not the vaguest idea about the stock market, foreign exchange, or even how a typewriter worked. . . . Had Max ever gone into a post office with Frank? After he'd written out a telegram and then tried to find out where to pay for it, going from window to window until he stumbled on the right one, paying no attention to *her* directions, then he discovered that the girl at the window had given him a crown too much in his change, and he returned it to her politely. But no sooner had he stepped outside the building than he realized the crown belonged to him after all; and now what to do? If he went back inside he—they—would have to stand in a long line; but it was unthinkable *not* to go back and put things right! It wasn't the crown, of course, but the principle. And the same sort of thing about money happened in every shop, restaurant, and in front of every beggar. Once Frank had asked a beggar for some small change for his two crowns. The beggar said he had no change, and so they stood around for two whole minutes while Frank considered what to do. And this was the same person who would unhesitantly and with happiness give her, Milena, twenty thousand crowns if he had them and she were in need; *but* if she were to ask him for nineteen thousand nine hundred and ninety-nine crowns, and he had to change money somewhere, he would hem and haw over how to work it so that she should not receive that extra crown she hadn't asked for! Above everything else was Frank's fear of losing his job.

Oh, how desperately she had needed to see him once, and had telegraphed, then telephoned, then written, pleading with him to come to her if only for a day. He had replied with loving excuses. Milena cursed him bitterly for those excuses. He spent sleepless nights and wrote her letters full of self-abasement, but he didn't come— because he couldn't bring himself to ask for the time off. He said he couldn't tell the director at the company that he wanted to come to *her*—and a lie was unthinkable, to this director whom he admired—especially for the way he could *type* so fast and well!

Milena, writing in her rapid, fluent, and passionate Czech, bared her soul to Max Brod. She admitted that she was too weak to break off completely with her husband; if she could have done this she was convinced that Frank would have come to live with her without the responsibilities of marriage. Yes, she was too weak; she needed the legal status of a wife, even with a husband who shamed her with his flagrant unfaithfulness! It was Frank who was the strong one, living his strict, ascetic life, with his lonely drive for perfection in all things.

Milena concluded that Frank did not have a real capacity for living in the world in which he found himself. He would never get well. Soon he would die, and there would be nothing she could do about it. In those words Max Brod heard the voice of heartbreak.

Twelve

THERE WAS A KNOCK at the door of Franz Kafka's office; he gave his customary "Please?" and the door opened to admit two visitors. They were father and son; the father was a fellow worker whom Franz especially admired because of his hobbies of carpentry and the making of violins. The son, age seventeen, was a budding poet, and his father had brought Franz some of his poems, saying jokingly that they were costing him a large electric light bill, since the boy was up half the night scribbling them.

Franz wasn't much impressed by the poems, but out of courtesy he asked to be introduced to young Gustav.

Recalling his first meeting with Franz Kafka, in 1920, Gustav Janouch remembered that Kafka had put out his hand and said, "You needn't be ashamed. I also have a large electricity bill."

Young Gustav had been nervously looking forward to meeting the published author of "The Metamorphosis," but at this greeting his shyness disappeared. He soon came to realize that Dr. Kafka, as he properly addressed this older man with a law degree, was not at all imposing, nor was he patronizing. Gustav got into the habit of falling in step with Kafka on his way home, to ask questions and make notes on his replies. The first note he was obliged to record was elucidating, if not complimentary. Kafka told him frankly that there was "too much noise" in his poems.

Thus began an account eventually to be called "Conversations with Kafka," which was to go on, sometimes with Franz's amiable compliance and at other times with his weary impatience, for the next three years.

Gustav's father had told him something about this strange and singular man. He would have liked to bake bread in his own oven and make his own clothes and furniture. He couldn't bear anything artificial, either in things or in people. Stock phrases aroused his suspicion. Convention, which he had permitted to surround him, he regarded as a mental and verbal uniform, a degrading form of prison dress. The elder Janouch, himself a man of great personal integrity, had never thought of his own office job in this way before, but he was honest enough to admit that it "fitted." Kafka, he added, was an individualist, a man who could not bring himself to share the burden of existence with anybody else, deliberately by his own choice a solitary. And in this respect, didn't his son Gustav see, Kafka was a nonconformist, an open militant?

A small incident in Kafka's office convinced Gustav of the truth of his father's words. The elder Janouch had come excitedly into the office to photograph a column of soldiers as they marched, with the band blaring, past the Institution. After they had passed Kafka had remarked offhandedly how boring a military parade was. Gustav's father reacted with surprise. Kafka said that modern armies had but one slogan: *Forward march on behalf of the people who sit behind us in power.* And thus, everything human and vulnerable was betrayed, including of course the men who made up the army. Gustav's father called him a rebel. Kafka said that unfortunately he was engaged in the most destructive and almost completely hopeless rebellion of all—against himself, his limitations and apathy; in the end, against his very desk and the chair he was sitting on. Then he gave a tired smile and tried to counter his irony with a few humorous remarks about their mutual business.

After he had left the office, Gustav's father burst out that, surely, that was just like Dr. Kafka! With a few words he could make you feel like a jack-in-the-box stuffed with empty phrases and opinions. But you couldn't blame him for it. And Gustav's father admitted that his photographing the military parade had been a piece of nonsense, deserving of no importance.

The elder Janouch also told Gustav about an old laborer whose leg had been smashed by a crane on a building site, and who was to receive only a paltry pension. He had brought an action against the Institution which was not in the proper legal form, and so would almost certainly have lost his case if Kafka hadn't stepped in and got him one of the best lawyers in Prague at his own expense. This put Kafka's own job in jeopardy, especially since the old man won his case, but that didn't seem to have even occurred to Kafka.

Young Gustav would drop into Kafka's office to be met by Franz, often having a coughing attack but cheerful in spite of it, as he tendered greetings from his "paper dungeon." Gustav offered to help him clear up the disorder on his desk but was met with a comically exaggerated protestation. If they were unlucky enough to straighten everything out, he, Kafka, would have no excuse to come back to work the next morning. Gustav, reading the insecurity behind the remark, reassured him of how much the company valued his services. Kafka's lighthearted reply was that he considered himself just a bit of expendable material. He didn't fall under the wheels of the bureaucratic machine, but only into the cogs, getting mangled a bit! This sort of thinking reminded Gustav of the operator of the torture machine in "In the Penal Colony."

To lighten the mood, Gustav remarked that his father called office work a dog's life. Kafka agreed with enthusiasm, adding that he did not bark at anyone, and didn't bite either. He was a vegetarian; and such people lived on their own flesh! At this, they both laughed so loudly that they didn't hear a knock on the door, and Herr Treml, sitting across the room with his permanent scowl, had to get up to answer it.

They strolled around the city after Franz had finished his work, sometimes through the park beside a small lake where there was a small group of white ducks. Watching the women and children buying bread from a lame old man with a white beard, and breaking it up to toss to the ducks, Kafka wondered who had the greater pleasure, the ducks or the people feeding them. Gustav thought it would be ducks because they received food, their means of survival. Kafka thought perhaps the people, who were consciously happy in the act of feeding them. Joy was food to the human soul, and without it life was only a form of dying. Kafka added that as a child he had derived great joy at being taken to a similar place to feed the ducks, except that his nurse usually teased him and pretended she would not take him so that, as often with his childhood experiences, it had been a mixed blessing.

Franz enjoyed the company of this younger, more eager mind, but that didn't prevent him from being perfectly objective in his responses. Gustav had admitted that he couldn't bear to be alone for more than two minutes at a time, a remark that shocked Franz, who couldn't bear it if he were *not* alone for a number of hours every day. And Gustav was reading everything he could buy or borrow, with what Franz felt to be uncritical enthusiasm.

He exclaimed with real alarm that Gustav's mind at present was "an absolute rubbish heap." Challenged, Gustav began developing a more critical attitude, and discovered the greatness of such writers as Balzac. From his own youth Franz had revered this lusty French lover of life and literature, on whose walking stick was the motto, "I break all obstacles." Franz confessed that on his own walking stick the motto should read that all obstacles broke *him*.

Gustav's father had told him about Franz's undeniably tubercular condition; and as Gustav could see, his mentor sat behind his desk, his face gray and drawn from coughing. But if anyone came in and inquired about his health he would reply almost with gaiety that he felt quite well. This struck Gustav as a conscious lie, and totally out of character for Kafka. He could not let this pass. Finally one day he got up his nerve and faced Kafka with it.

Franz at first tried to avoid the subject, then he gave in. He said that life itself is a drugged state, and that instead of walking ahead, one is really falling, falling from the moment of birth into the state of death. And so it's a direct offense to be rudely awakened out of this drugged state by an inquiry as to one's health. Gustav was alarmed, hearing Kafka's harsh, labored breathing. He said, with helpless goodwill, that Kafka might not be as sick as he thought, and in any event he should try not to think about his illness. This immediately struck Franz as funny, and he pointed out the impossibility of trying consciously *not* to think about a particular thing.

Gustav knew of Franz's love of carpentry and he invited Franz to drop in at his father's shop more often. He was abashed when Franz gently pointed out that he could no longer bear to inhale the sawdust that came from the fresh wood shavings, adding, "His Majesty the Body."

Yet Franz's mind was still as alert as this younger man's whose company he put up with and rather welcomed. No doubt one of the reasons he welcomed it was that Gustav's fresh, often brash and ingenuous questions gave Kafka an instant "platform" on which to perform— some small but acute observation that came immediately to the still-fertile mind yoked to a tiring body. Answering Gustav Janouch was a form of creativity that Kafka must have found less of an effort than setting down a short story.

Franz discussed with enthusiasm his admiration of ancient Chinese writings, especially the proverbs of Lao-Tzu in his quiet philosophy of Taoism.

> "The softest things in the world overcome
> the hardest things in the world.
> Nonbeing penetrates that in which there
> is no space.
> Through this I know the advantage of
> taking no action."

Another principle of Taoism that Kafka agreed with was:

> "The more laws and order are made prominent,
> The more thieves and robbers there will be."

He also pointed out to the avidly learning Gustav the principal work of another Gustav named Flaubert, *Madame Bovary*. Flaubert, said Kafka, almost as an aside to himself, had a tubercular father who had nevertheless gone ahead and dared to have a child. The reason for Kafka's mentioning Flaubert in the context of begetting a child was lost on young Gustav; Kafka was still in his anguish of correspondence with Milena Jesenká, still playing with the idea of marriage and fatherhood; but he said nothing to his young friend of his tormented relationship with Milena. Kafka added to his comments on tubercular writers by mentioning also Robert Louis Stevenson. The consumptive author of *Treasure Island* had at least escaped civilization by emigrating to the South Seas. Here was a late touch of Kafka's old longing to escape the harsh climate of Prague for hot, exotic countries such as Spain and Africa where, years ago, his uncles had resettled.

Gustav brought Franz one of the few reviews of his works, in which a critic, impressed with Kafka's use of animals speaking parables, had said that the author was a bird who fed on bitter roots. Kafka liked that, smiling and observing that animals were closer to humans than other human beings. He felt that it was a long distance between himself and the average fellowman. He was also depressed by the growing technology which, in 1922, had all but taken over Prague, a city which formerly had been associated with fine handcrafted work. Man, thought Franz, was fast becoming an outdated instrument whose economically inadequate skills would soon be displaced by thinking machines. Gustav objected: wasn't that just an idea out of a story by H. G. Wells? Answer: Wells was a good prophet!

Every famous man was grist for Kafka's mill; when the British imprisoned Mahatma Gandhi, Kafka said it was plain that Gandhi's movement would win, as his ideas would live by personal sacrifice. And there was the American, Walt Whitman. When the war between the Northern and Southern states broke out he had abandoned his role of romantic wandering poet to become a medical orderly. He had done what Kafka thought everybody should do in time of national grief—help the sick, the weak, the defeated.

In Gustav Janouch's account of his walks and talks with Kafka there is no passage more memorable than the one which describes the older man suddenly hastening down a steep cobbled street, hands buried in the pockets of his thin coat, with such rapid steps that Janouch, hardly coming up to his shoulder, had to make a determined effort to catch up with him. That must have been one of the days when Kafka's own tormented thoughts about his health, his writing, and his love were making it hard for him to be patient with this admiring young man who, he could see, was scribbling notes on his every word.

Around that time Albert Einstein, whom Kafka had admired when he was a professor at the university, published *The Meaning of Relativity*. Kafka wasn't particularly interested in Einstein's rather incredible theory which included such propositions as: "If you could travel to a distant star you'd find yourself younger than others on earth when you returned," but he did appreciate the joke that was making the rounds of the cafés about the Swiss-German-Jewish physicist: "If he is proved right in his theory, the Swiss will say he's a Swiss and the Germans will claim he's a German. If he is proved wrong, the Swiss will say he's a German and the Germans will say he's a Jew!"

Kafka was becoming more and more concerned with his own identity. Since he couldn't identify with being a member of his own family, or being either Czech or German, he had finally come around to working out and inquiring into his own history as a Jew. He recognized the deep and abiding need of Jews to go to Palestine, although he knew he himself did not have the mental and physical strength to uproot himself from Prague and make such a journey. One day, as Franz and Gustav were strolling past the Old Synagogue, Franz noted how the temple was dwarfed by the surrounding hills. And so, he thought, was everything Jewish; it was an ancient and alien religion. That was the reason for the hostile tensions that erupted into violent outbursts of aggression, as both he and Gustav had witnessed on the streets of Prague. The Jews wished to cut off their environment from the unknown by erecting their ghetto walls, but it had done them nothing but harm. Gustav agreed that having originally walled themselves in was foolish; the walls by now were gone, but anti-Semitism, the revenge of the shunned and despised Christians, remained. Kafka had a vision that the Christians would go further, in the not too distant future, and try to destroy the Jews entirely. Gustav was aghast and said he would never believe this. Kafka's face was sad. He added that this was only from his own point of view for, after all, he functioned in the insurance company as practically the solitary Jew, whom they all put up with as if he were a pet.

Soon thereafter Kafka was faced with a real problem from young Gustav: his father and mother were having terrible arguments. Frau Janouch, several years older than her husband, had, in middle age, lost all faith in her own attractiveness and was accusing her husband of being unfaithful. Gustav told Franz that both parents were demanding that he take sides; and he was afraid they would take a step which was almost unheard of at the time and carried with it an aura of scandal—divorce. (Later they took that step; and then within months, to Franz's grief, the carpenter and maker of violins committed suicide.)

The day that Gustav was so downcast at the impending

divorce of his parents, Franz took him for a walk across the beautiful old Charles Bridge with its famous statues; pointing at a little sandstone angel holding its nose between its fingers, Kafka remarked that it behaved as if Heaven itself stank; therefore everything on earth must have an even worse smell. Gustav walked on, downcast in his troubles. Kafka said something lightly about people being so lost and evil that this was probably the end of the world.

At once Gustav turned and challenged him. He did not believe it was the end of the world! Franz replied calmly but with a secret pleasure that a young man who didn't believe in tomorrow morning was a traitor to himself. In such a time one had to be gay. Didn't the ship's orchestra play to the end on the sinking *Titanic?* Besides, events were usually not as terrible as they appeared.

Gustav was not at all taken in by Franz's half-simulated cheer, and he said, "A forced gaiety is much sadder than an openly acknowledged sorrow." Perhaps it was at this moment that Franz Kafka came to respect the young man as a person in his own right.

They were nearing Kafka's father's place of business when Franz tried another tack. The trouble in Gustav's own home, he said, did not affect only him, he should try to stop feeling sorry for himself; his parents were even more distressed and humiliated than he was. They were in danger of losing the most valuable thing human beings could possess, their peace of mind. He, Gustav, should not reject and criticize them for their actions. On the contrary, he should try to give them as much support as they would accept, and that would return to them their self-respect. And how to do this? wondered Gustav. For Kafka, there was only one answer—by showing them a son's unquestioning love.

At that moment Franz and Gustav were passing the warehouse of Herrmann Kafka; and Gustav saw a heavy-set, middle-aged man come out of the building. He remained standing on the steps until the two had come abreast, and then he said, loudly, "Franz. Go home. The air is damp."

Kafka, reported Gustav, replied not to the man but to him, saying in a strangely gentle voice that this was his father, who was anxious about his health. "Love," he added, "often wears the face of violence." He parted from Gustav with an invitation to come visit him anytime.

Gustav went to see Franz at his rooms only once, and that was to bring him a book about a man who turned into a gigantic insect, which Gustav felt was a "steal" from "The Metamorphosis." Franz, ill in bed, waved his hand tiredly and said that the theme was far older than his own story. Some time later, Gustav took an extra job running the movie projector at a local theatre that was called *Cinema of the Blind,* and used the money to have three important published stories of Kafka's, "The Metamorphosis," "The Judgment," and "The Stoker," bound in a brown leather volume, with the author's name tooled in elegant gold letters.

Gustav, in modest pride and affection, told Kafka how he had earned the money by working in the cinema, then he presented the book to his friend. Kafka gazed at it in astonishment and chagrin; then he began to cough. After the attack was over he rather harshly said that the young man overrated him, and his scribblings did not deserve a gold-tooled leather binding; it was only his personal "specter of horror," and shouldn't be printed at all; in fact, it should be destroyed.

Gustav was furious with his revered author. How could he speak so slightingly of great writing? And the young man reminded Kafka of a remark he had made about the artist Picasso. Art was a mirror which, like a clock running fast, foretold the future. Well, said Gustav, perhaps his writing was, in today's *Cinema of the Blind,* tomorrow's mirror.

Kafka could not help but like that comparison; it was so like his own thought patterns. Then he summed up, remorselessly, his evaluation of his works. He said, "I am no light to the world. I've lost my way among my own thorns. For that reason, all my scribbling is to be destroyed after my death."

Gustav looked at his friend in horror and protest. Kafka leaned forward from his chair and addressed him, with infinite gentleness, by his nickname, Gusti. He spoke that day of the immensity of life, as far-flung as the stars above them, about which man had not even begun to guess; and that one man could only look at life through the narrow keyhole of his personal experience, and try to end up with a small statement about it. To make that observation true one had to be sure to keep the keyhole clean; and that was the sum of it.

Gustav Janouch went home to his then-divided family and wrote down the latest remarks of Dr. Kafka. And for the rest of his life, he tried to keep the keyhole of his own vantage point clean.

Thirteen

Nineteen twenty-three, and Franz had let his relationships with young Gustav Janouch and with Milena Jesenká languish, and then drop altogether. The walks and talks with Gustav had become too exhausting; so, too, were the letters back and forth between Vienna and Prague, with Milena begging for Franz's company. But Franz still saw his old friend Max Brod. Max was now a fairly well-adjusted writer of theatrical reviews and books of fiction. The three stories of Kafka's that interested Max most were "The Burrow," "The Hunter Gracchus," and "The Truth About Sancho Panza."

"The Burrow" concerned a small animal that had dug a house for itself in the ground, a snug and mazelike warren, to confound any predator that tried to get in. This was a silent and cozy place for the animal to live, alone and quite contented; but then there came a disturbance. The solitary occupant of the burrow could hear the breathing of some other creature—a soft, whistling sound. This faint but ominous whistling finally drove the burrow-dweller into a complete loss of his peace of mind. At least one contemporary critic of Kafka, a doctor, has come up with an ingenious explanation for this sound: "The healthy lungs are perfectly quiet; the tubercular lungs start up a whistling noise."

In another story that intrigued Max, "The Hunter Gracchus," a stranger, not quite dead and yet hardly alive, is deposited by a boatman on the shore. This mysterious man could be Kafka in his state of grave illness; or a symbolic Wandering Jew, as in "The Castle." It's of some interest that in this story Kafka was guilty of a small mistake, as if his attention were beginning to wander. At one point he has the boatman take the wrong turn and lose the way; and at another, he says that the boat has no rudder and is being driven simply by the wind.

A third story that, for Max, represented his friend at his lightest yet most memorable, was the little parable, "The Truth About Sancho Panza." In *Don Quixote,* the original story by Cervantes, Sancho Panza was the loyal servant of the Don who insisted on riding all over Spain righting wrongs. In Kafka's version, he assumes that each of us has his personal demon, or devil, who thinks up ways of tormenting us based on our own bad habits. Sancho Panza's demon is called Don Quixote, and he decides to get the better of him by charming and distracting him with stories of romance and adventure. The demon, taken in by these tales, goes forth to perform heroic deeds. Sancho Panza, relieved—and also suffering from a touch of guilt—lightheartedly goes along on the journeys.

Another piece of writing Max Brod was not to see until later was a letter the size of a small book that Franz had written to his father. It was a heartbreaking attempt to probe what was wrong with the relationship between Herrmann Kafka and his only son. Franz had given the letter to his mother to give to his father at some appropriate moment. Julie Kafka never found the appropriate moment; she said she thought it would upset her husband, and so finally she gave it back to Franz. Franz, in his never-ending attempt to show his father love, had dedicated his little book of *Contemplation* to Herrmann Kafka and handed him a copy. The elder Kafka received it with gruff embarrassment, put it on his bedside table, and never mentioned it again. And *still* Franz butted his frail, sick head against the indomitable fact that his father was an utterly different sort of man from himself. He wrote in his diary that he did not care what his family thought of him; the world was wide, there were other courts of appeal. And in the same breath he admitted that without his family's approval the judgment of the outside world was as nothing.

He sought approval in that world, and the world, almost to a man, approved of him; still he could not approve of himself. As his young friend Trude Thieberger was to point out years later:

> "It was Goethe, whom Kafka admired so much, who coined the formula, 'May none think himself capable of overcoming the first impressions of his childhood.' "

Fourteen

IN THE SUMMER OF 1923 Franz was staying with his sister Elli and her children, Felix and Gerti, in a seaside resort on the Baltic Sea. There he came upon a holiday colony of the Berlin Jewish People's Home which fired him with enthusiasm. At one time he had persuaded Felice Bauer to take part as a voluntary helper in the work of the home. Now, years later, he met children from there on the little beach and played with them.

One day Franz noticed a girl in the Home's kitchen; she was energetically scaling fish. Franz, the vegetarian, said with disapproval that a girl with such gentle hands should not be engaged in such a bloody business. The girl was startled, but attracted sufficiently to this thin man with the intense gray gaze that she asked to be assigned to other work. Thus began the friendship between Franz Kafka and Dora Diamant.

Dora was only about twenty at the time, and had run away from her little Polish town and Orthodox Jewish family with their rigid customs, and come to Berlin, where she was studying art, literature, and Hebrew at the high school. Franz, who had always wanted to learn Hebrew, was easily persuaded by Dora to enroll.

There he met Dr. Friedrich Thieberger, a teacher of Hebrew and the brother of Trude Thieberger. Franz had become embarrassed about the way he was coughing in classes, and so he begged the teacher to give him private lessons. For a description of Kafka at this school there is none better than that contributed by Dr. Fritz Bamberger, now a professor in New York but then an impressionable student.

"His appearance created quite a stir. Not because we young students crowded around the famous writer. Kafka was not famous then. He was known only to a few and there was no one available to identify to us the newcomer as the author of *The Penal Colony,* or another of his few slim volumes. . . . The special attention which Kafka received stemmed from the fact that he took his seat at a library table which, though it provided room for five or six readers, was traditionally reserved for a sole occupant. This single occupant zealously and belligerently safeguarded his unofficial prerogative against any and all invaders. A young and promising scholar in Talmudic literature . . . he needed lots of space for his voluminous tomes, and the end of the table, just where Kafka had seated himself, was used by him each noon to lay out on a neat piece of paper his monotonous lunch, bread and *Harzer Kaese* [Harz Mountain cheese, stronger-smelling than Limburger]. Such culinary use of the library was not in accord with regulations, but all our protests against the odoriferous concomitants of his frugal meal . . . had been of no avail. But Kafka won without argument. And that was the sensation. Whenever he came up to the library, on days when he felt relatively well . . . a man of forty, sitting together with boys just out of high school, the disputed chair was his. The Talmudist scholar muttered, 'Weird fellow!' and took his lunch to a deserted classroom."

Franz was happy studying Hebrew at the school with Dora Diamant. Dora was quiet and unassuming; she was eager to learn what Franz could teach her of literature and travel. He, for his part, drew her out as to her knowledge of Hebraic history and customs. And Dora did not bring up the subject of marriage. Franz felt himself relaxing with this simple yet intelligent young woman. He came back from his summer holiday deciding to sever all ties with Prague, go back to Berlin, and live with Dora.

And perhaps for the first and last time in his life Franz Kafka did just what he wanted to do. He left Prague at the end of July, went to Germany, and set up housekeeping with Dora in spite of his family's objections. He wrote Max Brod that for the first time in ages he felt happy and was even sleeping well.

At first the couple lived in a Berlin suburb where they were obliged to contend with a landlady whose moral disapproval led to their moving out—and Franz wrote a story about "A Little Woman," who was constantly at war with her own ego. Next, the pair found an idyllic place in a charming villa run by a lady doctor. Max Brod visited Franz and Dora there, and to his gratification heard Franz remark that his personal demons had finally lost track of him.

Franz and Dora, attending the school where they were studying Hebrew, came under the affectionate but worried attention of the librarian, Fräulein Jenny Wilde, of whom Fritz Bamberger says: "Jenny Wilde was no shining light as a scholarly librarian. It was almost touching how hard she tried to cover up her professional weaknesses. She never conceded that there was a book she did not know. She made us believe that she had read them all, including those nonexisting ones whose titles we dreamed up. But here was a warm and motherly heart. Her instinct told her when a student was in need. She knew how to win confidence and give aid—counsel, food, money, anything—to an aspiring young man without humiliating him. . . . She took a hopelessly torn shirt home for repair, and when it came back, it was miraculously new, even bore the label of her favorite store in the Frankfurter Road, where she bought at a discount.

"Dora Diamant was one of her protégés. Fräulein Wilde was truly fond of her, admired her struggle for independence. . . . But she was deeply worried that Dora lived with a sick man. . . . Two of 'her' students were living together! . . . They were members of an academic institution, a theological school, in fact, whose principles were not exactly conducive to Bohemian living. . . . So Jenny Wilde sat down and wrote a letter. . . ."

The librarian had got it into her head that Dora's

autocratic Orthodox father was the only obstacle to a marriage between Dora and the sick young man she obviously was in love with, so she wrote an earnest letter to him, and showed it to her student helper, Fritz Bamberger, "in strictest confidence." Some of the young man's confusion shows up in his later account: "I was to judge whether this was the right way to broach the matter to a pious Hassid. Never was there a more incompetent expert!" Apparently young Bamberger's diffidence was enough to give the librarian second thoughts, for it is doubtful the letter was ever sent.

Despite his failing health, Franz was in fine spirits. After all these years he had finally severed his relationship with the Workers' Accident Insurance Institution, and he could hardly believe it had really happened. Somehow, he would earn a living in another way. He was out in the brisk autumn air of Berlin every day, breathing deeply and talking himself into a return of vigor and health. One day in a city park a little girl of about eight came up to him, crying that she had lost her doll.

"Oh, you haven't lost her," Franz said. "She has just gone on a little trip!"

The child looked up at him in doubt; so Franz got her name and address and wrote her two or three letters, and then bought a doll and mailed it to her. She wrote back to him that "It has changed." Franz's reply: "Well, that's what travel does to people!"

He wrote his sister Valli an exuberant letter in which he cheerfully, if with his customary wryness, told her of his daily confrontations with the wall calendar in his apartment. It had a little motto or saying for each day, and

Franz chose to take this motto to heart. One day he had an idea for a short story which seemed full of significance, so he consulted the calendar's motto to see if it "agreed." To his chagrin and amusement the message was, "Even a blind dog finds something sometimes!" an old German proverb.

The summer-autumn idyll turned, inevitably, into winter; and a bitter one it was. The aftermath of the 1918 war was still being felt in 1923, and inflation had rendered the mark practically worthless. In Germany people talked of little else but the "index figure," the figure of how much a German mark was worth every morning. One got on the streetcar before noon for 15,000 marks; after noon it cost 30,000. The usual greeting between friends was: "How are you?" with the reply being a kind of multiplication: "Rotten—times the index figure!"

He stubbornly insisted on managing for himself and Dora on the dribble of royalties that he received from his few published efforts, and the tiny pension he had begun to receive from the insurance company. He didn't want to accept money or parcels of food from his family, although they were sending them up to Berlin. Franz's main thoughts were of paying back his family debts, money he had accepted from his father, little as it was, and in return, sending expensive birthday presents to everybody. He directed one of his sisters, a member of a Prague Jewish women's club, to send gift parcels to the really poverty-stricken in Berlin. Then he happened to examine one such parcel, and found it to be filled with nothing but the bare necessities of life—without a square of chocolate or an apple—as if the parcel were saying to its recipient,

"Here is just enough food to keep you alive for a week longer."

Rice, flour, sugar, and coffee were the staples of the food parcels; the same staples on which Franz and Dora lived that winter in Berlin. He decided that they would have to give up one of their two small rooms the next month to a boarder. Everything was cooked on their tiny gas stove; they declared they would not dare get "sick," although Franz was coughing badly; but despite all this Franz said cheerfully that if he and Dora could just find jobs as waiter and cook in a restaurant everything would turn out fine.

Nothing turned out fine. At the end of the winter Max Brod came to Berlin and took Franz back to Prague, to stay in his parents' house. A week later Dora followed, with a mutual friend, Dr. Klopstock. Klopstock was a young medical student, himself a tubercular patient, who worked at a sanitorium as a male nurse.

Lying in his old room in his father's house, Franz and Herrmann Kafka looked at each other, and somehow began to draw closer together. Franz had given his father a copy of the memoirs of Benjamin Franklin, as the relationship between the young Franklin and his father had been so much warmer than Franz's with his own parent. This hint fell on deaf ears, as the senior Kafka, handing back the book to the bedridden son, muttered something about "Suppose you gave me this because he was a vegetarian, eh? Well, I'll never be." Yet Franz lay in the narrow bed of his childhood and counted the things he remembered that had brought him close to his father. There was a hot summer afternoon, or perhaps several of them, when Franz used to see him, tired after lunch, dozing at the warehouse office with his elbows on the desk. Or when he went with Franz, his mother, and sisters to the country for a little fresh air. Or when Franz's mother was dangerously ill and his father had clung to the hall bookcase, shaking with silent sobs; or when—most poignant moment of all for Franz—Herrmann Kafka had gone softly to his room to see him during his latest illness, and stopped at the door, stuck his head in and, out of consideration for the sick man, only waved a hand.

By the beginning of the long, bitter winter of 1924 Franz was again steadily coughing blood, and over his protests he was taken to a sanitorium. On the 10th of April the sanitorium's doctors, having diagnosed tuberculosis of the larynx, deemed it necessary that he be sent to a Vienna clinic.

There was just one car available for the journey, an open convertible. The day was cold, windy, and rainy. All through the journey, Dora Diamant stood up in the car trying to protect Franz with her body against the rain and the wind. Robert Klopstock, too, proved his loyalty. To accompany Franz on this sad trip he broke off his studies in Berlin, which were later to lead to important research results in the treatment of the lungs. These two, Dora and Dr. Klopstock, now referred to themselves playfully as Franz's "little family." They both knew it was an intimate sharing of their affection with a doomed man.

Finally, at the end of April, Dora and Robert Klopstock succeeded in having Franz transferred from a rather gloomy institution to a friendly, light-filled sanitorium in a suburb of Vienna called Kierling, where they got him settled in a lovely room filled with flowers and overlooking the green countryside. Franz was in pain but optimistic. He said that if he ever got well he would like to marry Dora, and he had sent her Orthodox father a letter stating his intentions.

According to Max Brod, this was Franz's last real push toward living. He followed the doctor's instructions perfectly and without protest. He really seemed to be ready at last to consider the thought of being married. Dora, with her rich knowledge of Jewish history, suited him perfectly, and he knew he had much to give her of his knowledge of the whole body of literature. They shared fantasies, and laughed and joked like children.

But the pain mounted; it clutched at Franz's throat, especially when he coughed. Soon he began to call out to Max, trying to make poetic allusions to his agony, calling the pain "the tightening straps of the suitcase," which he had often put over his shoulders, in preparation to going on a vacation trip with Max. But now the straps, the pain, were tightened more and more, and still the trip—his death—was not taken.

He became very thirsty but it was becoming harder for him to swallow; and—perhaps this was typical—he urged others clustered around his bedside to partake of beer, wine, and fruit juices. He said that just watching them drink these liquids gave him a satisfaction of sorts.

On another day, however, he grimaced with pain. He was his old self, ironically humorous: What a long time it seemed to take before one was crushed up quite small and squeezed through the last narrow hole! Finally he began to cry out to Robert Klopstock for the relief of morphine, which Klopstock had promised him.

His arms raised, the emaciated Kafka cried: "Now, don't cheat me! Kill me, or you are a murderer!"

The young doctor, overcoming his own emotions, administered a heavy dose of the narcotic, and Franz thanked him, but soon asked for more. Finally he went into a drugged sleep.

His last words were about his sister Elli, with whom he'd spent the last summer with her children. Klopstock was holding his head. Kafka imagined it was Elli he saw instead of his doctor friend, and by then he was terribly afraid he might infect somebody. And so he cried out for Elli to move away from him. Klopstock moved away a little and that seemed to pacify the dying man.

Just before Franz died he made a gesture of total rebellion. An ice pack had been bound around his head; with his remaining strength he tore it off and threw it on the floor. As Klopstock turned away from the bed to clean a syringe, Franz whispered, "Don't leave me."

His friend answered that he was not leaving him.

Franz said, in a deep voice, "But I am leaving you."

On Tuesday, June 3, 1924, Franz Kafka died in the Kierling Sanatorium. He was not quite forty-one—*a man of ethereal refinement of spirit and crystal clarity of mind, a poet whose fame will only be experienced by posterity, a Jew of deepest bonds with Judaism.* . . . That was a portion of one obituary in the Prague newspapers. Another obituary printed, in its entirety, the story, "Before the Law," later to become a part of the book, *The*

Trial. Perhaps no other writing of Kafka's could have been more fitting in the summing up of his life.

Before the Law, said Kafka, stands a Gatekeeper. To this Gatekeeper there comes a man from the country and asks politely to be let inside. The Gatekeeper says he cannot grant admission at the moment. The man thinks it over and then asks if he will be allowed in later. The Gatekeeper says this is possible. The man decides to wait, and the Gatekeeper gives him a stool to sit on, beside the open gate. There he sits, for days and weeks and years, making many attempts to have the Gatekeeper change his mind, all to no avail. As he grows old he grumbles to himself, and finally his eyesight begins to fail. Yet in his darkening view he is now aware of a radiance that streams from the gateway of the Law. Now he knows he is dying. He has one last question to ask. "Everyone strives to reach the Law," he feebly whispers. And so how does it happen that for all these years nobody but himself has ever begged to be admitted?

The Gatekeeper replies that no one else could ever have been admitted to this gate, since it was made only for this one man. And now, at the end of his life, he is obliged to shut it.

Fifteen

ON THE DAY of the funeral the sky was overcast and foggy with a threat of imminent rain. A small group of Franz's friends had come, riding or on foot, to the Jewish cemetery of Strašice, in a suburb of Prague (even in death Kafka was to be segregated as a Jew). There were Dora Diamant, leaning on the arm of Franz's oldest friend, Max Brod; blind Oskar Baum, Trude Thieberger, whom Franz had taken to *Carmen;* and Trude's husband, Johannes Urzidil. Urzidil was also to write about his late lamented friend: "The majestic towers of the city with its bridged river were no longer visible." Each member of the group had bent over and brought up a handful of earth to toss upon Kafka's coffin, as was the custom. "I remember this earth exactly," Urzidil wrote. "It was light-colored, lumpish, clayish, permeated with little stones and pebbles."

Pebbles! Max Brod, walking back from the funeral in the misty rain, may have remembered Franz's birthday gift to him, away back in 1908. Two books and a pebble; the books, Franz had said, might be lost—but if Max lost the pebble it could be replaced by picking up "the next best" pebble Max found on a path. But Max had kept the original pebble.

Eight days after the funeral a memorial service was held in the Little Theatre in Prague. This was attended by the same group of friends with the addition of Kurt Wolff, Franz's publisher, who was to go out of that meeting hall and the next day begin to call the attention of the world to the genius of Franz Kafka.

At the service Johannes Urzidil spoke:

> "How can we, a generation of very unstable values, carry away with us more . . . lastingly this model who has thrust himself so powerfully upon us than by making him an effective part of ourselves? . . . A new and better heart seems to be growing for us in our attachment for this man, Franz Kafka . . . who bears witness to us of his compulsion for truth. . . . He had only a single guideline, that only he who persists till the end can be blessed."

And then the people of Prague opened their newspapers to find the final obituary of Kafka, by a young journalist who wrote in passionate Czech and whose name was Milena Jesenká:

> "He saw the world as a place full of invisible demons waiting to tear and destroy human creatures. He was too

wise and clearheaded to cope with life. . . . His works are the most significant in modern German literature; they are free of slogans, but they reflect the struggles of today's generation everywhere. . . . All his works are full of the sense of hidden misunderstandings, of human beings wronging each other without blame. Both as a man and an artist his sensibility and anxiety were such that he perceived dangers where others, whose senses were duller, thought themselves safe."

And, after Franz's death, what happened to his works; and to the friends and relatives he cherished, whether or not they deserved it?

Shortly after the funeral Gustav Janouch received a small present from the cleaning woman who worked in his father's house in the morning. Afternoons Frau Svátek worked in the Accident Insurance Institution. She presented Gustav with a beautifully hand-painted porcelain cup and saucer that, for years, Franz had used for tea, and which Herr Treml had been about to throw out. As she gave Gustav this memento of Franz she was voluble with her memories. He had been so different from other people. One could see it in the way he gave you something. Other people would hand it to you in such a way that you would feel humiliated. But Dr. Kafka—for instance, a bunch of grapes he had not eaten that morning —Dr. Kafka never left them looking like leftovers, but would arrange them tastefully on a plate, and then entreat her, did she think that she could possibly make some use of them?

Gustav agreed with the cleaning lady with fervor. Kafka had the art of giving. He never said, "Take this, it's a present," but when he gave a book or magazine: "There's no need to give that back to me."

Young Janouch was very moved by the gift, and thanked Frau Svátek for her thoughtfulness. The little porcelain cup accompanied him throughout his life, although he had too much reverence for its original owner to use it to drink from.

It was to be another eight years before it would occur to Gustav Janouch to do anything about the journal he had kept on Kafka; and then he sent his efforts to Max Brod.

Max, meanwhile, had been given another sort of present, one that he found far less welcome than Gustav's cup and saucer. This was a piece of paper in Franz's desk addressed to Max and saying specifically and firmly that upon the occasion of his, Franz's, death, Max Brod was directed to seek out all stories, diaries, notebooks, and letters he might have left, and burn them, preferably without reading.

There followed a period of soul-searching on the part of Max Brod. Should he go against the wishes of a man who no doubt knew he was dying? Did Franz really want the labors of his creativity destroyed, or was this request the self-pitying, dramatic posing of a sick man? Max remembered how Franz had referred to his stories as the only children he would probably ever have.

And at another time Franz had spoken in his odd, strange-angled way, of the "real" life of a book beginning only after the death of its author; even quite a while after his death, for sometimes the author will eagerly go on fighting for his book in some sort of spiritual agony; but finally the book is on its own, and then it relies only on the strength of its own pulse, its honest worth.

Such intense feeling about his writing, Max felt, could just not be equated with Franz's command to burn all his labored efforts. Of course it was apparent from the beginning of his dilemma that the world had the right to read the output of this extraordinary writer. But that was not Max Brod's main concern. What he was after, in desperation, was to do what Franz Kafka would really have wanted.

And then he thought, had Kafka not destroyed other papers that he felt should not be preserved—for instance, the bulk of letters from his first fiancée, Felice Bauer? With this evidence it was obvious that Kafka himself had burned letters that he did not want to survive him; and he had not burned his own literary efforts.

That evidence was not very strong, but it was enough for a good friend who wanted with all his heart to disobey the dictates of a writer whose works he vastly admired. And so he got up from his desk, assembled the unpublished stories and books of "F. Kafka," and went to the publishers of Prague.

It wasn't an easy task. He had to leave one manuscript with one publisher, one with another. But the following year, 1925, *The Trial,* was published. The next year, *The Castle* appeared. Neither caused any great excitement. Max tried to get editions published in Germany. He was met with contemptuous denial from the postwar, anti-Semitic government. The name Franz Kafka was obviously Jewish.

Next, from Vienna, Milena Jesenká began to correspond with him. Then she sent him the diaries that Franz had entrusted to her; and finally his letters. As with Felice Bauer, Franz had destroyed Milena's letters to him.

Later came news about a former friend of Kafka, Grete Bloch. Grete had come from Berlin on her pilgrimage to Kafka's grave, and from there had written to a mutual friend of Max Brod that she had given birth to a child by Kafka, a son, who had died in Munich in 1921 at the age of seven. She stated her facts calmly as if she only wanted to set the record straight. Brod was so moved by this news that he neglected to ask the name of the child, and he was never to learn it, for shortly thereafter Grete Bloch fled the Nazis from Berlin to Switzerland, then to Italy, where she was captured. Later evidence had it that she had said or done something to enrage a German soldier, who had clubbed her to death with his rifle butt.

Brod couldn't leave it lightly—how might the knowledge of Franz having fathered a son have changed Franz's life? Would he not have been delighted—along with his automatic fear of responsibility? Perhaps having a child would have "straightened him out," or would it have thrown him into a worse emotional panic than he had ever been at the very thought of marrying. All is speculation, in fact, even the evidence of a son ever having existed is open to speculation; yet the testimony of Grete Bloch, so casually reported, does carry the ring of truth.

Kafka's influence first began to be felt in France, from whence it spread to England. By the early 1940s and in spite of the outbreak of World War II, newspapers and magazines were praising the creative output of the young

Czech writer who, they said, had been far ahead of his time.

America was next. By 1950, when volumes of Kafka's collected works began to appear in Europe, American critics were hailing them as belonging to world literature. "Kafka is the greatest of the moderns," they declared; and compared him further to Dante, whose *Divine Comedy* was a breakthrough for literature. For his clear vision and sinewy prose he was compared to Shakespeare, whom Kafka so revered; and to the great philosopher-writer, Goethe. Thereafter the rush was on to praise this hitherto unknown middle-European Jew, and among the voices raised were those of Hugh Walpole, Aldous Huxley, Arnold Bennett, André Gide, Hermann Hesse, Martin Buber, Thomas Mann, Franz Werfel, and many others in German, French, Dutch, Czech, Polish, Italian, and Hebrew, uniting, as Max Brod wrote, in explaining Kafka's importance.

Such praise, however, was not quite unanimous. For instance the celebrated American critic Edmund Wilson felt that Kafka's neuroses made him a second-rate writer, and chided him in print somewhat testily, for "his little-boy-like respect and fear in the presence of the boring diligence of commercial activity, the stuffiness of middle-class family life, and the arid reasonings and tyrannous rigidities of Judaism—" this last, at least, a condition that Kafka was never tyrannized by.

In the 1970's critics and readers agree that Kafka's message is peculiarly relevant. "We find emphasized time and again the similarities between Kafka's world and the

grotesque menace of events in our own lives. . . ."
"Kafka reflected the chaos of modern civilization when bureaucracy ignores the human, the individual." "Kafka speaks to the alienated, not in comfort perhaps, but as a fellow sufferer."

What, one wonders, was the reaction of Franz's father, Herrmann, and his gentle, obliging mother, Julie, who lived on into the years when their son was acclaimed a writer of great talent? Apparently no one bothered to interview them and get their opinions. They died shortly after smiling obligingly into the camera as the parents of their surprisingly famous son, and were buried in the same cemetery in Prague.

All three of Franz's sisters, Elli, Valli, and Ottla, were captured by the Nazis and sent to Hitler's concentration camps, where they died.

As for Milena—having left her husband in Vienna at a time when he had four mistresses, she returned to Prague to write about the impending holocaust. As critic Arthur Koestler wrote: "She helped Jews and fellow countrymen to escape. She published an illegal magazine and called for resistance to the oppressors. After a short time she was arrested by the Gestapo, and sent to Ravensbrück where she died in 1944."

Jenny Wilde, the librarian who vowed she had read the books whose names were made up by her teasing students, was also sent to a concentration camp. Miraculously she survived. In 1945 her former student, Fritz Bamberger, contacted her to see if he could send her anything essential, such as food. She could not think of any special food package in her state of mind. "I sent her, among some other things, a ballpoint pen," said Dr. Bamberger—a gift Franz Kafka and any other writer, intent on keeping his sanity, would have appreciated more than bread and rice.

Two years after Franz's death the military authorities of Prague contacted the surviving relatives. They were, they said, still trying to track down "Kavka, Frantisek," in order to issue his "Certificate of Discharge" from the army. The relatives were surprised and confused. Since Franz had been a civil servant he had never been drafted.

That incident prompted Max Brod to remember a boyhood picture of Franz, in which he was depicted with his head thrown back and his mouth open, laughing with a boyish abandon at some nonsense he had heard in the sober, pontifical world of adults.

It was with that kind of laughter, a kind of innocent delight at the incongruities of bureaucracy, that Franz Kafka might have greeted the arrival of his Certificate of Discharge from an army he had never joined.

His death was his Certificate of Discharge. His stories will go on living "relying on the strength of their own pulse," so long as there are readers to read them, to enter the dreamlike dimensions, rooted in earthly matters, of the strange and special world that was Franz Kafka's.

TINLEY PARK HIGH SCHOOL
TINLEY   ILLINOIS
LIBRARY DISTRICT 228

Chronology

1883 Franz Kafka is born, July 3, in Prague.

1889–93 Attends grammar school in Prague.

1893–1901 Attends high school in Prague.

1901–06 Attends the University of Prague. Studies law.

1902 Begins friendship with Max Brod.

1906 Works in uncle's advocate's office, Prague. Summer in Trest with Dr. Löwy. Writes "A Country Doctor" and "Wedding Preparations in the Country."

1907 Works in an Italian insurance company. Writes "Description of a Struggle."

1908 Leaves the Italian office and begins work at the Workmen's Accident Insurance Institution.

1909	Two sections from "Description of a Struggle" published. Vacation with Max Brod.
1911	Begins his diaries. Meets the Yiddish theatre troupe. First trip to Paris with Max Brod.
1912	Meets Felice Bauer. Writes "The Judgment," "The Stoker" (first chapter of *America*) and "The Metamorphosis."
1913	*Contemplation* published. Also "The Stoker." Trips to Vienna and Venice.
1914	Becomes engaged to Felice Bauer in Berlin and breaks it. Writes "In the Penal Colony" and begins work on *The Trial*. War is declared. (Kafka, a civil servant, is not obliged to serve.)
1915	Again meets Felice Bauer. Receives the Fontane Prize for "The Stoker." Leaves his parents' house to live alone.
1916	At Marienbad in July with Felice Bauer. Changes his residence.
1917	Second engagement to F.B. in July but breaks it in December. Is informed of a diagnosis of tuberculosis. Is granted sick leave from his place of work. Begins the study of Hebrew.
1918	Works on *The Great Wall of China*. Stays with a sister at Zürau.
1919	"A Country Doctor" and "In the Penal Colony" published. Also Kafka writes the *Letter to His Father*.
1920–23	Letters to Milena written (later to be published under this title). Spends the winter in a sanitorium in the Tatra Mountains. Writes first draft of *The Castle*.

1923	Meets Dora Diamant. Manuscript of *The Castle* in the care of Max Brod. Kafka lives with Dora Diamant in Berlin, Kafka begins "The Burrow," "Josephine the Singer," "A Hunger Artist."
1924	Kafka returns to Prague with Max Brod. Dying, Kafka is taken to the sanitorium in Kierling. He dies on June 3, and is buried in the Jewish cemetery of Strašice.
1925	*The Trial* is published.
1926	*The Castle* is published.
1927	*Amerika* is published.
1931	Previously unprinted stories are published.

Bibliography

Bauer, Johann. *Kafka and Prague*. New York: Praeger Publishers, Inc., 1971.

Brod, Max. *Franz Kafka, A Biography*. New York: Schocken Books, Inc., 1963.

Janouch, Gustav. *Conversations with Kafka*. Translated by Goronwy Rees. New York: New Directions, 1971.

Kafka, A Collection of Critical Essays. Edited by Ronald Gray. Englewood Cliffs, N.J.: Prentice-Hall, Inc., 1962.

Kafka, Franz. *Amerika*. New York: New Directions, 1946.

————. *The Castle*. New York: Modern Library, 1969.

————. *The Diaries of Franz Kafka 1910–1913*. Edited by Max Brod. Translated by Joseph Kresh. New York: Schocken Books, Inc., 1948.

————. *The Diaries of Franz Kafka 1914–1923*. Edited by Max Brod. Translated by Martin Greenberg with cooperation of Hannah Arendt. New York: Schocken Books, Inc., 1948.

————. *Letter to His Father*. New York: Schocken Books, Inc., 1966.

————. *Letters to Milena*. New York: Schocken Books, Inc., 1962.

————. *Selected Stories*. With an Introduction by Philip Rahv. ("The Judgment," "The Metamorphosis," and "In the Penal Colony," etc.) New York: Modern Library, 1952.

————. *The Trial*. New York: Random House, 1969.

Urzidil, Johannes. *There Goes Kafka*. Detroit, Mich.: Wayne State University Press, 1969.

Index

« 181 »